REFLECTIONS ON DEATH, DYING AND BEREAVEMENT

A Manual for Clergy, Counselors, and Speakers

William A. Smith

Death, Value and Meaning Series
Series Editor: John D. Morgan

Baywood Publishing Company, Inc.
AMITYVILLE, NEW YORK

Baywood Publishing Company, Inc.
26 Austin Avenue
Amityville, NY 11701
(800) 638-7819
E-mail: baywood@baywood.com
Web site: baywood.com

Library of Congress Catalog Number: 2002019811
ISBN: 0-89503-270-8 (cloth)

Library of Congress Cataloging-in-Publication Data

Smith, William, 1929-
    Reflections on death, dying, and bereavement : a manual for clergy, counselors, and speakers / by William Smith.
        p. cm. - - (Death, value, and meaning series)
    Includes bibliographical references and index.
    ISBN 0-89503-270-8
    1. Death. 2. Bereavement. I. Title. II. Series.
BD444 .S57 2002
128'.5- -dc21   2002019811

This book is dedicated to my dear sister-in-law,
Judy Comeau Talarczyk,
whose final illness did not allow her to
"go gentle into that good night."

Table of Contents

Preface vii

Acknowledgments ix

September 11, 2001 xi

Introduction 1

CHAPTER 1
Human Immortality 5
    Supplementary Texts 8

CHAPTER 2
The Problem of Evil and Human Suffering 15
    Supplementary Texts 19

CHAPTER 3
Reflections of Philosophers, Novelists, Poets, and
Other Writers on Life, Death, and Immortality 25
    Theistic Philosophers 26
    Atheistic/Agnostic Philosophers 34
    Pagan Philosophers 38
    Novelists, Poets, and Other Writers 41

CHAPTER 4
Grief and Bereavement 55
    Death of a Husband 57
    Death of a Wife 57

Death of a Child 58
Death of a Parent 60
Death of a Sibling 62
Suggested Readings 64
Supplementary Texts 64

Appendix I. Suicide and Euthanasia 75

Supplementary Texts 79

Appendix II. The Hospice Movement 83

Appendix III. The Funeral Director 85

Conclusion 87

Bibliography 89

Index 95

Preface

This manual has seen the light of day thanks to a sabbatical leave granted by Seton Hall University for the spring semester of 1998. My thanks go to Dr. David O'Connor, chairman of my department, who encouraged me to work on this subject and wrote letters of support to our then acting dean, Jo Renee Formicola, and our former provost, Dr. Bernhard Scholz, both of whom also gave their support for this effort.

Over the past five years, I have taught Seton Hall's Philosophy of Death course four times. This has given me an acquaintance with the literature in this area of philosophy. My sabbatical allowed me the time to examine philosophers' (first and second level), novelists', and poets' thoughts on death in greater detail.

Every class in the Philosophy of Death course has invited an administrator from the hospice movement and morticians who explained their role as "funeral director." I took copious notes from these guest speakers, and some of that information is included in this book. I hope the reader can benefit from it.

Chapters 3 and 4 are, I believe, the most important for my readers. Nevertheless, many people question the purpose of the amount of physical and emotional suffering we are forced to endure, and many wonder about the continuation of some kind of life after death. Perhaps philosophy/reason can come to our aid when faith is tested. This is the reason for Chapters 1 and 2. Each chapter contains extracts from and discussions of texts that illustrate and supplement the topics of that chapter. In Chapter 3 these are integrated into the text; in the remaining chapters they follow my main discussion, under Supplementary Texts. Chapter 4 also contains a short list of Suggested Readings that may prove of practical value in assisting the bereaved.

I have not included Asian philosophies in the book because I am not all that familiar with them and I believe that the distinction between philosophy and religion is not too sharp. Inclusion would also make the book larger than I want it to be.

Clergy and counselors must also deal with the subject matter included in the Appendices, so I hope these will also be helpful.

Acknowledgments

Many persons should be mentioned who have contributed to this book in various ways. Certainly Dr. Jack Morgan, Editor of the *Death, Value and Meaning Series,* who has advised on content and given encouragement over the past three years.

I would like to thank the Rev. Frank McNulty, Dr. Dianne Traflet, Dr. Frank McQuade and Dr. David O'Connor for their thorough reading of the text and their valuable suggestions.

Special thanks must go to Pat Gallagher, M.A., who encouraged and assisted me in a variety of significant ways, including research on the Internet and in libraries, interpreting my handwriting, and toiling throughout many months of "drafts" and "fine tunings" before arriving at the final product.

In the final hectic months of dealing with changes and permissions, Pat and my secretary, Ms. Diana Violaris of Seton Hall helped me put the finishing touches to the book.

Finally, I owe a debt of gratitude to my wife, Joyce, who encouraged me to persevere throughout the last five years and did some of the initial editing and proofreading of the book.

September 11, 2001

On the day of the terroristic attacks on the World Trade Center in New York City and the Pentagon in Virginia, this book was basically finished. Were I to re-do the book, many allusions could be made to these attacks and the "massive death" which resulted.

In re-viewing my book, I noted that death by war is often mentioned. There are of course many different species or types of war. We now find the world in a war against "terror" aggravated by the altruistic type of suicide which Durkheim and Alvarez explain in my Appendix on suicide. The United States is now firming up its "Intelligence War" capabilities.

The strain of funerals on families and clergy has been enormous. It is my hope that the reflections in this small book will serve to offer some degree of easement as well as consolation to anyone who might read it.

May God grant His eternal presence to the victims of terrorists everywhere and give the strength to cope and endure to all the bereaved.

Introduction

Death practices in the United States are placing great demands on the time and energy of the clergy. At hospitals everywhere, clergy minister to the dying and their families. Both Protestant and Catholic clergy, including deacons and parish coordinators, are expected to attend wakes, preach at funerals, and, perhaps, accompany the family to the gravesite, where some final words of comfort will be offered. In the ensuing days and weeks, additional family counseling may be deemed necessary. At least two events among the many tragedies of 1996 demonstrated to me that there might be a need for a guide or manual to assist these functionaries in such situations.

At a funeral Mass for a police officer killed in the line of duty, the parish priest opened his homily by saying that he really *did not know what to say* about the officer's death. It is my belief that the question must be posed: Is it not part of this priest's vocation—or profession—to give this man's relatives and friends some explanation or analysis of the mystery of evil and suffering in the world? In another case, a former priest-author admitted in a book that he had never been trained to deal with people in a state of deep grief. His first wake was a disaster at which the young widow, mother of several small children, verbally attacked him because he could only think to ask, "How do you feel about this?"

Please understand, I am not saying that I, or any human for that matter, have solved the mystery of death and suffering. Clergy who must deliver a homily and speakers at memorial services face a daunting task. They themselves might be almost overwhelmed by a specific tragedy.

After the dormitory fire at my university (Seton Hall, January 19, 2000), a memorial service was held for the three students that died. Many words were spoken, and it is true that the emphasis was on faith and trust in God's wisdom and love when trying to understand the mystery of the death of the young. Nevertheless, I am simply trying to show that this is a topic that humans have pondered and written about for centuries, and in this book I try to convey to speakers and even teachers some of these reflections.

The methodology of this short treatise is mainly philosophical. It is intended to complement scriptural and theological studies. I will leave to others the selection of relevant texts and authors in those areas. I am not discarding the consolation that comes from religious faith and divine revelation; rather, I am simply taking a different approach.

Unfortunately, in cases of suffering and tragic death, religious faith can be shaken and severely tested. Many people are only "nominal" Christians or Jews whose faith is weak and biblical knowledge marginal. Being told that it is "the will of God," while of course ultimately true, is not a satisfactory explanation for tragedy in the view of many people.

It is my hope that this guide will give clergy another source to fall back upon to supplement the religious. Many of the greatest "first level" and "second level" philosophers of the Western world as far back as Socrates and Cicero have meditated and written on the mystery of human suffering and death.

Twentieth century psychologists, psychiatrists (including Freud), and sociologists have made contributions from their own sciences. Novelists and poets have addressed the subject. Death and its results for the living come in many different ways and combinations. I hope this short compendium will be of service to a harried clergy, "other speakers," and eventually, if enlarged, will serve me and perhaps others as a textbook for thanatology courses.

My eight years as a seminarian in a Catholic religious congregation noted for its preaching ministry prepared me for a public speaking career as well as for the administration of the Sacraments and a clerical life. More than thirty years of teaching, research, and attendance at wakes and funerals prepared me to write this book, and while I have heard homilies on death at wakes and funerals of all the major religions, I have never heard a sermon on death at a Sunday Mass.

This led me to the conclusion that perhaps clergy wait until the dying process or death to broach the topic to survivors and family members. We hear people complain that the clergy do not talk about sin and hell anymore because they do not want to upset anyone. Could this be the same reason that few, if any, preach on the mysteries of terminal illness and death?

Is it not true that we are a society that is almost in denial concerning death? We do everything possible, societally speaking, to slow down the aging process: health food stores, vitamin supplements, strenuous exercise, dieting, and face-lifts—the list could go on and on. I am not necessarily "putting down" these efforts, but I think they should not totally detour us from an awareness of the destiny we all face.

Even pagans, atheists, and agnostics have the courage to think and write about the inevitability of death. I would think, therefore, that people who believe in God and personal immortality could tolerate and survive a sermon on the topic.

Clergy should prepare their people to come to grips with the fact that relatives and friends will probably precede them in dying and death and that they themselves will one day have to endure it. The exit from this life can be sudden and easy or lengthy and painful, both physically and emotionally. If doctors such as Sherwin Nuland (1995), author of *How We Die,* are right, the dying experience is lengthy and unpleasant for some if not most people. His book contains a chapter that might be of interest, "Doors to Death of the Aged," in which he describes the seven major "entities" that make up the "posse" that hunts down and kills the elderly.

Clergy should pose the question, "Why do we have to die?"—not what are the physical reasons, but rather why is it part of God's plan for the human race? I think we all know some of the usual answers. We were not made for this world alone. Our ultimate destiny or end is supernatural: "enjoyment" of the beatific vision (God) for the "rest of eternity." We have to make room on earth for new life. Since matter is intrinsically corruptible, a vital organ must sooner or later break down.

The part of that last statement that often presents a problem for the clergy is not the "later" but the "sooner," since the death of the elderly does not represent a great mystery for most people. The mystery lies rather in at least two phenomena: the death of the young and the *manner* of death (terminal cancer, accidents, war) of people of any age.

Therefore, a sermon (or better yet a series of sermons) on dying and death demands some reflections on the problem of evil, human suffering, and the mystery of the will of God. Granted, these are among the greatest mysteries for philosophers and theologians, but this is no reason for clergy to ignore them. Some explanation is owed to the members of the religious community or other groups, even if it is, in the final analysis, inadequate. Clergy are supported by people who have a right to expect not only consolation on an emotional level, but some reason or reasons on the intellectual level. The serenity of the weekend "service" is a far better venue than a hospital room or wake.

CHAPTER 1
Human Immortality

The belief in a life after death, be it from religious faith or logical deduction, has been a source of consolation to the dying and the bereaved since the early days of Christianity and even, longer ago, among the ancient Egyptians. This "afterlife" concept can involve various rewards and punishments, depending on the religious belief. Christians see it as more spiritual ("presence of the beatific Vision— God"); some Muslims see it as involving physical pleasures. Many hope to be united once again with dead relatives, ancestors, friends, or, as Socrates hoped, famous personages (the *Apology*).

Technically, the duration of this afterlife would be aeviternal, that is, a life that had a beginning (therefore not eternal) but will have no end (therefore not temporal). Some have speculated about the possibility of God's eventually annihilating (moving from being to nothingness) all human souls. Reason would allow for such a possibility, although Christian revelation would seem to hold for everlasting happiness or even punishment. Most feel that if the soul is intrinsically capable of unending existence (is not corruptible), it would seem unreasonable to destroy it. As religious persons we would certainly hope for eternal life with God, and with Augustine we pray for the gift of faith: "Lord I believe; help thou my unbelief."

However, what is the clergyperson to do when faith fails someone? What if he or she is asked to give and explain the reasons for his or her own faith—meaning rational arguments rather than the professed faith of the individual? The clergyperson usually does not have the advantage of a calm, unemotional setting, as does, for example, a classroom lecturer. Interrogation by grief-stricken family members or even by the dying person can take place in a hospital, at a wake, or when surrounded by relatives at a post-funeral gathering. These situations can be very tense and filled with high emotion.

Therefore, let me briefly outline the approach of "rational argument" to this presentation of immortality. First, a fact: corruption of the body begins immediately after death. This disintegration can be staved off temporarily by the embalming process, refrigeration, and the airless condition of a coffin. Nevertheless, the brain and nervous system have ceased to function. If the afterlife involves acts of knowledge (conscious use of intellect) and acts of love (functioning of the will, now in the presence of God), then something other than the brain must be the source of intellectual and voluntary operations. If I am nothing more than my body, then at death "I" (my "self") am finished. Immortality can be had only through my actions (e.g., works of art, music, or literature) or my children; but there can be no consciousness of personal survival because there is no personal survival. Thus immortality, survival of consciousness, requires some aspect or factor of my being to be other than physical or material, not subject to corruption or disintegration after death. The history of philosophy gives us terms like "psyche," "soul," or "mind" to represent this part of our human makeup. Platonists believe that this combination of psyche and soma (the body) is a union of two separate entities (or substances). Strict Aristotelians would see it as a duality of co-principles making up the one human being.

A student once asked me whether any kind of survival after death is possible if there is no God. I must admit that I had never fully reflected on this question, but I think we would have to say that if one's soul is a finite, contingent entity, it would necessarily have to come under the power of some cosmic force in order to be preserved in existence. Humans know this "force" that conserves the "finite" universe by many names, but I think the existence of this Being must be accepted. Never open Pandora's box unless you can reclose it!

I would divide the argument for the spiritual soul into two general types or approaches: the traditional and the nontraditional. The *traditional approach* considers the characteristics of physical beings: physical/material entities are quantified, measurable, divisible. The laws of physics restrict them to one area of space at any single moment of time (spatial-temporal limitations). Physical beings are big, rough, smooth, hard, soft, dark, and light. The brain, which materialistic philosophers believe is "the mind," fits these characteristics. However, another type of reality does not fit: namely, ideas. Ideas or concepts, such as love, beauty, and justice, have no size or shape or weight. They are immaterial: they have only meaning. The question is, can brain cells have not only an understanding of justice, or love of neighbor, but also a *concern* about these virtues? And what about free will? If the mechanistic concept of the human person is the true one, then we are nothing more than flesh-and-blood "machines." But machines such as car engines and computers are not "free." True, we have instinctive "drives," like sex and hunger, which are a result of having bodies, but these drives can be controlled because their purposes are understood by our power of reflection and we *acknowledge* a moral law. We can reject sexual temptations, but animals cannot. Humans diet or reject cholesterol-laden foods for the higher good of their own health.

To summarize: we have conceptualization, recognition of the moral law, freedom from some mechanistic laws of matter, and the power of reflection. Many people do not believe the brain, as magnificent as it is, can be the *fully* adequate cause of these powers in humans.

By the *non-traditional approach* I mean the use of extrasensory perception (E.S.P.) phenomena and "near death experiences." E.S.P. phenomena include mental telepathy, clairvoyance, and precognition. Mental telepathy, the transference of thought from one person's mind to another's without the use of words or signs (speech or writing), bypasses the Aristotelian epistemological/psychological theory that all knowledge begins in the senses. Clairvoyance is also knowledge, but knowledge of *events* that have taken place beyond the range of the "naked" senses and knowledge gained without artificial means such as radio. If this power really exists, it is a transcendence of the space and place limitations of matter. Precognition is real knowledge of future events. This would be a transcendence of time limitations, because the future area of time has, as yet, no reality. It is difficult to determine how many reports of these events are authentic. One could check the writings of Drs. J. B. Rhine and Louisa Rhine, formerly of the Duke University Parapsychology Laboratory. This transcending of the space-time limitations of physical being would seem to indicate a nonphysical power source within us and therefore something incorruptible. The famed English philosopher Bertrand Russell (see Chapter 3), was somewhat impressed by these investigations but nevertheless did not accept the existence of a spiritual soul.

In his book *Life After Life*, Raymond Moody, M.D. (1975) brought to light the phenomenon of what is perhaps, finally, some empirical evidence of the survival of a soul. Moody deals with stories of people who have clinically (not irreversibly) died and been resuscitated. After resuscitation, these people reported autoscopic experiences (out-of-the-body experiences, which involve looking down or back at medical personnel working on one's body), meeting dead relatives, seeing a very bright light at the end of a tunnel, and, for some, undergoing a judgment of their life (which most said was conducted in a friendly atmosphere—a part of the experience that I certainly hope is authentic).

Although Moody admitted that all the cases mentioned were not of the same scientific and investigative rigor, he must be given credit for making a beginning and opening himself up to criticism.

Other studies in this area were done by Michael Sabom, M.D. (1982), in *Recollections of Death*. And a comparative study of some Americans and some Indian sub-continent Hindus was done by Karlis Osis, Ph.D., and Elendur Haraldsson, Ph.D. (1977), in *At the Hour of Death*.

In conclusion, while we know that these "arguments" do not convince everyone, they are certainly worthy of consideration and expanded study. If memory serves me right, a respected Jesuit Gregorian University cosmologist once paraphrased Shakespeare: "There are more things in heaven and earth, Aristotle, than were thought of in your philosophy."

SUPPLEMENTARY TEXTS

Twenty-Third Psalm

Surely goodness and mercy shall follow me all the days of my life; and I will dwell in the house of the Lord forever.

The Roman Ritual (used in the Catholic funeral service)

May the angels lead you into Paradise, may the Martyrs receive you at your coming and take you to Jerusalem, the Holy City. May the choirs of angels receive you . . . and may you have life everlasting.

St. Thomas Aquinas (1225-1274): *Summa of Theology* (*Summa Theologica*) (1894 Latin edition)

Whether the Human Soul is Something Subsistent?
I answer that . . . the principle of intellectual operation which we call the soul of man, is a principle both incorporeal and subsistent . . . able to understand the nature of all bodies . . . it is impossible for the intellectual principle to be a body . . . for it to understand by means of a bodily organ since because of the determinate knowledge of a specific organ . . . it would not be able to know all bodies. . . .
Therefore the intellectual principle which we call the mind or the intellect has an operation proper to itself in which the body does not share . . . we must conclude therefore, that the human soul . . . is something incorporeal and subsistent (I, q. 75, a. 2, c).

In article 6, Aquinas concludes that "everything that has an intellect naturally desires always to exist"; and that "a natural desire cannot be in vain. Therefore, every intellectual substance is incorruptible."

This question from the *Summa of Theology* philosophically complements the famous text from the first letter of Paul to the Corinthians:

> For the trumpet will sound, the dead will be raised incorruptible, and we shall be changed. For that which is corruptible must clothe itself with incorruptibility and that which is mortal must clothe itself with immortality . . . then the word that is written shall come about: "Death is swallowed up in victory. Where, O death is your victory? Where, O death is your sting?"

H. D. Gardeil, O.P. (b. 1900): *Initiation a la Philosophie de St. Thomas d'Aquin—Psychologie,* Vol. III (1956).

> The soul, however, has no composition of matter and form or of any constituent parts. The soul is pure form, utterly simple, having its own act of existence. . . . Of its very nature, then, it is incorruptible, which is to say immortal (p. 227).

Curt J. Ducasse (1881-1969)

Professor at Brown University, in his book *A Critical Examination of the Belief in the Life After Death* (1961), Ducasse makes his famous distinction between the physical and the psychical: "things called 'material' . . . are perceptually public or can be made so" (p. 40); "events, processes, denoted by the term psychical or 'mental' are the inherently private ones . . . thoughts, emotions . . . volitions" (p. 45).

Although Ducasse set the stage for the traditional "arguments" for immortality he chose a different route. In a May 1947 lecture entitled "Is a Life After Death Possible?" he concludes:

> To the present writer, as to McTaggart,[1] it does seem that if survival is a fact, then the plausible form it might take would be *rebirth* on earth, perhaps after an interval occupied by the individual in distilling out of the memories of a life just ended such wisdom as his reflective powers enabled him to extract. And this conception of survival also seems to be the one which would put man's present life on earth in the most significant perspective [emphasis in original].

Aristotle (384-322 B.C.): *De Anima*

> Turning now to the part of the soul with which the soul knows and thinks. . . .

---

[1] John McTaggart (d. 1925), British metaphysician, Hegelian Idealist, who held that individuals are immortal and are rewarded through *reincarnation*. (For more on the subject of reincarnation, see the section "Near Death Experiences" later in this chapter.)

Thus that in the soul which is called the mind (by mind I mean that where by the soul thinks and judges) is, before it thinks, not actually any real thing. For this reason it cannot reasonably be regarded as blended with the body; . . .

. . . while the faculty of sensation is dependent upon the body, mind is separate from it (Bk. III, Ch. 4).

Note: There is no unity of interpretation of Book III, but one must wonder: if Aristotle rejected Plato's "World of Forms/Ideas," what would we do in the next world?

Plato (427-347 B.C.): *Phaedo* (Socrates), "World of Ideas"

And now, O my judges, I desire to prove to you that the real philosopher has reason to be of good cheer when he is about to die, and that after death he may hope to obtain the greatest good in the other world. . . . Do we believe that there is such a thing as death? . . . Is it not the separation of soul and body?

Your favorite doctrine, Socrates, that knowledge is simply recollection . . . would be impossible unless our soul had been in some place before. . . . here then is another proof of the soul's immortality.

Charles Sanders Peirce (1839-1914)

American philosopher, logician, mathematician. Peirce's doctrine of "Synechism" was the doctrine that all that exists is continuous and therefore rules out the ultimate dualism between mind and matter: "What we call matter is not completely dead, but merely *mind* hidebound with habits" (6.102).

In an 1881 passage he wrote, "The one intelligible theory of the universe is that of *objective idealism,* that matter is effete *mind,* inveterate habits becoming physical laws" (6.25).

Note: "Effete" here means worn out. See also 1.436 on material bodies having a psychical substratum. Quotations are from *The Collected Papers of Charles Sanders Peirce,* 8 volumes (Hartshorne and Weiss, 1931).

Sir James Jeans (1877-1946)

English astrophysicist. In his book *Physics and Philosophy* (1942), Jeans distinguished the "man-sized" world from the conceptual world of subatomic physics:

These conjectures [of science] were often good enough for the man-sized world but not . . . for the ultimate processes of nature which control the happenings of the man-sized world, and bring us nearest to the *true nature* of *reality* (p. 190).

Arthur Eddington (1882-1944)

English astronomer and investigator of relativity physics. In his book *The Philosophy of Physical Science* (1939 and 1958), Eddington dealt with the relationship between the physical (objective) and psychic (subjective; i.e., the world of consciousness, free will, non-determinism, values, or basically idealism). With regard to subjectivism, he tells us that "it is right to say that Kant . . . anticipated the ideas to which we are now being impelled by the modern developments of modern physics." (I imagine he is referring to the mental constructs of the structure of the atom.)

PARAPSYCHOLOGY AND
NEAR DEATH EXPERIENCES

Rather than accept the view of some type of idealism—namely, that perhaps the material world is actually closer to the characteristics of ideas than to those of physical being—parapsychologists usually accept the mind-body dualism. Their tendency is to reject a strict monistic materialism or spiritualism and to conduct research on the power of the mind. Their primary mission is *not* to demonstrate the continuation of conscious life after death, even though psychic research had its origins in investigative research on "mediums," seances, and spiritualism.

Years before Joseph Banks Rhine and his wife Louisa Rhine joined Prof. William McDougall, the distinguished British psychologist who had moved from Harvard to Duke University, many famous persons became interested in seance claims and conducted investigations. Among these were William James (1842-1910) and Harry Price (1881-1948), who wrote *Fifty Years of Psychical Research—A Critical Survey* (Price, 1975) (the 1939 edition is in New Jersey's Rider College library). Other famous persons involved in this were Sir Arthur Conan Doyle (1859-1930) and Lady Jean Doyle; Conan Doyle worked with Sir Oliver Lodge (1851-1940), an English physicist who helped develop radio, but later became deeply interested in spiritualism. Conan Doyle, although most famous for the Sherlock Holmes mysteries, also wrote *The Wanderings of a Spiritualist* (1921) and *The Edge of the Unknown* (1930). He was once the president of the London Spiritualist Alliance.

Conan Doyle preferred spiritualism to religion. John Dickson Carr (1906-1977), in his book *The Life of Sir Arthur Conan Doyle* (1975), relates Conan Doyle's view: "It did not hurl perdition right and left, or tell a man his soul was lost over a point of doctrine." (Conan Doyle attended a strict Jesuit school called Stonyhurst (high-school level).

Price (1975) remarked that "spiritualism is, at its best, a religion; at its worst, a racket!"

Before we look at some quotations from the Rhines at Duke, let me mention another university famous for this research—the University of Utrecht. Price mentioned that the British Broadcasting Corporation informed him of a Dr. W. H. C. Tenhauff, whose lectures on Dutch radio on psychic research were very popular.

Joseph Banks Rhine (1895-1980)

J. B. Rhine was director of the Parapsychology Laboratory at Duke University until the early 1960s, and from 1965 was director of the Foundation for Research on the Nature of Man (FRNM). In his book *Parapsychology from Duke* to FRNM (1965) he tells us:

1. The third main impression of the field of Parapsychology to which I draw attention . . . is the impression that the research findings of this field are making sense. . . . It was pointed out in one of the papers that all types of psiphenomena[2] showed the same non-physical character . . . (pp. 107-108).

Rhine (1956) stated that "so long as telepathy itself was a poorly established hypothesis it did not provide a very strong counterargument to spirit communication [spiritualism, mediums]"; this "gave the investigation of it a new importance and led in the early thirties to the Duke experiments in E.S.P." (p. 123). Further,

The mechanistic (or physicalistic) view of man has become the mental habit of the student of science. . . . [But] out of these researches has now blossomed a concept of the nature of man that seems to approach the criterion of spirituality . . . (pp. 123-126).

Louisa Rhine (1891-1983)

While J. B. Rhine dealt mainly with the experimental laboratory work (testing subjects, assessing statistical data), his wife concentrated on extra-laboratory, spontaneous cases and "field" reports. She called this the "anecdotal" approach. Some of her conclusions are given in her book *The Invisible Picture* (1981). The "set of unique circumstances [McDougall and Joseph Banks Rhine coming together by accident at Duke] helped the field of parapsychology to develop as the more general experimental investigation of the evidence for a non-mechanistic aspect of human nature" (p. 10). It has shown that "the objective world is not totally hidden to the human psyche by space and time because psi ability

---

[2] Telepathy, clairvoyance, precognition, psychokinesis.

transcends the limited sensory faculties" (p. 247). "Case studies were scattered over . . . fifty or more years . . . [and] each had kept alive . . . the idea that psychic occurrences represented an unexplained human phenomenon" (p. 249).

NEAR DEATH EXPERIENCES

Probably the original (or even "classic") book on the subject was Raymond Moody's *Life After Life* (1975). Moody was a graduate of the University of Virginia and a former philosophy professor.

> At the present time I know of 150 cases of this phenomenon . . . and for some fifty persons they were resuscitated after having been thought, adjudged or pronounced clinically dead by their doctors (pp. 16-17).

Some had autoscopic experiences and others met "guides" to assist their transition to the next world.

From Kübler-Ross's foreword:

> It is also corroborated by my own research and by the findings of other serious minded scientists, scholars . . . and clergy. . . .

Kübler-Ross feels that it has required a certain amount of "courage" for these professionals to investigate these claims. I have read that she herself has risked her credibility by claiming to have had some contact with deceased individuals whom she refers to as her "spooks."

Osis and Haraldsson (1977) spoke of dying persons "seeing" someone with a "take-away purpose" or mission. In their pilot study *not* a single apparition involving a phantasm of a *living* individual was described as coming with the take-away purpose (p. 91).

On the fringes of these investigations that search for more empirical evidence of immortality we find *reincarnation*—the return to another body (*carnis*, Latin for flesh). Readers interested in these claims should research the data from the University of Virginia School of Medicine and Division of Parapsychology, whose director was Dr. Ian Stevenson. I am aware of one extraordinary case this group was investigating when I worked in Washington around 1958.

If I recall correctly, the *Washington Post* ran a story concerning a young girl in Eastern Pennsylvania, about ten years old, who could speak a language no one could identify. It was not German or "Amish." A recording was made and sent to the foreign language department of several universities. It seemed to be a northern European language, perhaps Scandinavian. I have never seen a follow-up.

Curt Ducasse, in a final section of his book *A Critical Examination of the Belief in a Life After Death* (1961), outlines in greater detail both his and John McTaggart's conception of a theory of reincarnation. Ducasse (1961, Chapt. XX) concentrates on Metempsychosis and defines it according to W. R. Alger, a "learned Unitarian clergyman," as "the notion that when the soul leaves the body it is born anew in another body, its rank, character, circumstances and experience in each successive existence depending on its qualities, deeds and attainments in its preceding lives." Ducasse then tells us of various views sympathetic to this belief, namely those of Brahminism, Pythagoras, Plato, Plotinius, and others, including David Hume (1711-1776) who stated it to be the only doctrine on immortality that "philosophy can harken to." However, Ducasse's next chapter (1951, Chapt. XXI) deals with "difficulties" with the reincarnation "hypothesis."

CHAPTER 2

The Problem of Evil and Human Suffering

Anyone who has had a good training in theology or philosophy is aware of the so-called "problem of evil" and the classic "statement" of it. Nevertheless, it probably would not hurt to refresh the memories of some and perhaps present the problem to others for the first time— at least the problem as *I* perceive it.

The dilemma concerning evil exists if we acknowledge at least two things: (1) the existence of God and the traditional concept of Him; and (2) the existence of death and human suffering in the world. Life experience teaches us of the second, and either faith or rational argument, or both, convince many of the first. Therefore, the classic statement of the problem could be put as follows.

If God is (a) infinite (unlimited) in power (omnipotent); (b) infinite in the knowledge of His creations (omniscient); (c) infinite in the possession of the virtues we find (albeit to a finite degree) in humans, such as justice and mercy; and (d) a loving "parent," how can He possibly cause, or even tolerate, the human suffering that results from tragic death, painful diseases, and emotional traumas?

Here, obviously, we are attempting to navigate the realm of mystery. To paraphrase Frederick Copleston, let's at least try to identify the nature of the mystery. In what does it lie? How can we "penetrate" it?

To do this, most philosophers begin with a definition of evil. Evil, it could be stated, does not possess true existence. This is because we define evil as a "privation," an absence of a positive perfection or power that should be present in an entity because of the very nature of the entity we are considering. It is, as some say, "due" to it.

For example, vision is a positive perfection. Humans and some animals should naturally possess it. Therefore, blindness is a physical evil in a human or a dog, an absence of a power that should be present. Death is the absence of life (although it might not always be an evil in my opinion, and proper distinctions would have to be made with regard to life being "due" to us).

Physical evil is one of the three types of evil usually identified by philosophers and theologians. The second type is *moral evil*—the absence of obedience to the moral law; in theological terms, sin. For example, murder is the killing of another person when we lack the *right* to kill. The third type of evil is called *natural evil*. Examples of this type would be earthquakes, hurricanes, or tornadoes, which cause death and destruction of property.

As you can see, our problem is one of reconciliation. How can we reconcile this existence and great numbers of occurrences of these three types of evil throughout the ages with belief in a God, who, if all-powerful, could stop the evil and, if truly a loving parent, would do so? If eternally omniscient, He must have known these tragedies would take place, and if just, why has He allowed *the innocent* to suffer?

For clergy this has always been one of the most difficult dilemmas to explain as part of their ministry. Television coverage constantly presents us with images of the funerals of police and firemen, the remains of servicemen brought back from war, crying widows and children. Sometimes, however, the very presence of clergy and friends gives great emotional support to the grieving. At the Seton Hall memorial service I mentioned earlier, the relatives and friends of the dead and injured were surrounded by five thousand people including bishops, politicians, emergency personnel who gave assistance at the fire, faculty, administrators, and local citizens. Also, the view of Augustine and Aquinas that an all-good God will bring some good out of evil is confirmed when we see the examination of safety features in dormitories throughout the nation. Incidents of false alarms are also down in many colleges. Hopefully, all this is of some consolation to the bereaved.

Responses and defenses can be provided in the calm atmosphere of a classroom or Sunday service, but these will probably prove to be less than adequate for someone in a state of deep grief. At such a time, the faith of some people is terribly shaken, or simply lost. I have read that the Holocaust caused Elie Weisel to lose his Jewish faith. I once taught an American-born Jewish woman who never suffered personally in World War II but was unable to reconcile the horror of the Holocaust with the traditional notion of a loving God. On the other hand, her friend who was a "survivor" and had lost all her family still practiced her religion. She believed with Augustine that some "good" *did* come out of it, namely, the state of Israel—this thanks to the sympathies of many throughout the world.

Let us now consider some responses or explanations that might be given to people who are seriously disturbed by the suffering they have witnessed or heard about.

St. Thomas Aquinas, the great medieval theologian/philosopher, admits his inability to understand the suffering of the innocent. In the Prologue of his *Commentary on the Book of Job* he states that nothing is more difficult to reconcile with divine providence than the suffering of the innocent. I shall return to this in the next chapter.

In his *Summa of Theology* (I, qq. 48-49), Aquinas tells us that while God tolerates moral evil because He gave us free will, He could never cause it, although He might cause physical evil for a good reason. Along these same lines, Aquinas quotes St. Augustine's *Enchiridion* at the end of his "Fifth Way" (*Summa,* I, q. 2, a. 3), answering his own first objection to the existence of God. Augustine taught that because God's goodness is infinite, He could only allow evil if some good should come from that evil. In his commentary on *Job,* Aquinas returns to this.

Aquinas's approach in the *Summa* is rather technical and, therefore, I would recommend a perusal of his *Commentary on the Book of Job* also.

It seems to me that St. Augustine's view demands great faith that in the "long run" matters will turn out favorably; eventually, we will understand.

We all know that when we talk about God, we often find ourselves resorting to analogies. Following up on Augustine's view, one analogy I like to see is derived from a situation in which combat officers often find themselves. Just as we mortals try to comprehend God's plan for us, so military personnel are often perplexed by higher command decisions. Junior officers might not know why the colonel (a regimental commander) has given them seemingly inexplicable orders, but they must have faith that the colonel knows the reason for the orders. It is possible, of course, that even the colonel does not understand what is behind the orders, but he must trust the generals who perhaps see the "overall" situation of a war being conducted in various parts of the world.

Religious people often face the same problem as the military of various ranks. Their faith is tested. Hopefully they will come to realize that *their* lives and the lives of those around them are part of a divine plan that is working itself out in conjunction with their own free choices.

Some say that God does not love us. He cannot possibly be a "loving parent." But are love and suffering incompatible? Of course not.

Parents sometimes let their children suffer. They withhold privileges or permissions; they may use a variety of disciplinary measures; they may even allow their child "to learn the hard way" in not-too-serious matters. The question has at times been asked: Is God our heavenly Father punishing us? Recall that Aquinas held that God might cause physical evil but never moral evil.

"I have no problem with God dealing justly with evil-doers, but many sincere people do pose the questions which are raised in Rabbi Harold Kushner's famous book: *When Bad Things Happen to Good People*. He mentions that he is often approached, even at parties, by people who are "troubled by the unfair distribution of suffering in the world" (p. 6).

Is there any "morally sufficient reason" for God tolerating the adult human behavior which causes so much suffering? (In his book *God and Inscrutable Evil* (1998), Professor David O'Connor terms these sad situations "gratuitous evil.")

To return to my analogy: loving parents do punish wrongdoing and potentially dangerous behavior, and I believe that, if done with moderation, it is not only a right but even a duty of parenthood. However, one hopes that the *motive* for causing this suffering and disappointment is *love,* concern for the child's welfare, present and future. Most children eventually understand the reasons for their parents' actions.

In order to defuse this dilemma, some philosophers resort to the concept of a "finite God," that is, a God who is not infinite in one or more of the "attributes" we traditionally assign to Him, such as omnipotence. Philosophers with a deistic bent will exaggerate God's transcendence: He has set the laws of nature in motion and has withdrawn to His heaven. Others might feel that when certain terms are predicated of God, such as "loving" or "just," our understanding of them is equivocal not analogous.

It is true that these beliefs would help explain the various evils. I believe we should press on and continue to analyze the mystery as classically presented. I think William James of Harvard considered this solution.

I would like to return to the problem of moral evil. Here the blame is usually attributed to humans themselves for the abuse of the great gift of free will. This is a profound and complex issue. It can involve the question of predestination, God's control of every action in the world, and, theologically, the question of eternal punishment.

The problem as I see it is, could God have made earthly creatures who would be superior to the animals without endowing them with intellect and free will? I do not think so. However, our intellects are finite. Our judgments and decisions are fallible and often uninformed, selfish, or, to be blunt, just plain dumb. Our will chooses from among the options presented by the intellect together with its evaluations. Even in the case of natural disasters (which, by the way, follow certain laws of nature, hence there is not really "disorder" here), humans are sometimes responsible for their own sufferings. We have damaged the environment and the ecosystem; we are to blame for shoddy construction; human error has been involved in many maritime disasters; we have built human habitations in dangerous areas; we have not taken note of predictably dangerous weather situations—the list could go on.

Human hatred, greed, and desire for power have caused suffering to millions. And yet, if we were to have free will, God had to take this risk. Freedom always involves risk, such as the child's first solo drive with the family car. Therefore, if God's eternal decisions are immutable, He is not going to control the internal act of the will. If people choose to sin, this will be permitted. This is one aspect of the "will of God." It is permissive.

They say President Harry Truman had a sign on his desk that read, "The buck stops here." God created man free and thus we have the conundrum: moral evil exists because God allows it to exist. We might even ask whether God has put a limit on His own power, if, by an eternal decision, He cannot change an evil will. God can only do what can be done.

I have tried to provide here a variety of reflections on the presence of evil in the world. God has given us many "gifts" and things to enjoy, but He never promised us perfect health and happiness. He does not "owe" us a life without sorrow.

We can come up with many explanations for evil, but in the final analysis it will probably remain a mystery. Why? Because God is a mystery.

SUPPLEMENTARY TEXTS

St. Augustine (354-430)

City of God, XII, 3 (1950)

On moral evil:

> In Scripture they are called God's enemies who oppose His rule, not by nature but by vice; having no power to hurt Him, but only themselves (p. 382).

> It is not nature, therefore, but vice which is contrary to God. For that which is evil is contrary to the good . . . to God no evils are

hurtful; but only to natures mutable and corruptible, though . . .
originally good (p. 382) [Modern Library, New York, 1950].

Enchiridion, XI

As quoted in St. Thomas Aquinas (*Summa of Theology,* I, 2, 3, ad. 1),
on evil in general: "Since God is the highest good, He would not allow
any evil to exist in His works, unless His omnipotence and goodness
were such as to bring good even out of evil."

Moses Maimonides (1135-1204): *The Guide for the Perplexed* (Completed in 1190), Pt. III, Ch. 12 (Baird and Kaufman, 1997)

> Men frequently think that the evils in the world are more numerous
> than the good things. . . . they say that a good thing is found only
> exceptionally. . . . God is perfect goodness. . . . and that all that
> comes from Him is absolutely good. . . . we suffer from the evils
> which we . . . inflict on ourselves. . . .

Maimonides goes on to describe three kinds of evil caused by illness,
or assaults of some sort, which come from others and those for which
we ourselves are responsible due to poor choices. These choices (free
will) usually stem from some excess of the various physical, sensual
pleasures.

St. Thomas Aquinas

Literal Exposition on Job

From the "Prologue":

> Although the opinion of the majority of man was confirmed in
> the belief that natural things were driven not by chance but by
> providence because of the order which manifestly appears in them,
> doubt emerged among most men concerning the actions of man. Did
> human affairs proceed by chance, or were they governed by some
> providence or superior ordinance? . . . for good things do not always
> happen to good men or bad things to bad men. On the other hand,
> neither do bad things always happen to good men or good things
> to bad men. . . .
>
> Now what especially seems to impugn God's providence where
> human affairs are concerned is the affliction of just men . . . that just
> men should be afflicted without cause seems to undermine totally
> the foundation of providence. Therefore, there are proposed for the
> intended discussion (quaestio) as a kind of theme the many grave
> afflictions of a certain man, perfect in every virtue, named Job.

Note: In order to support his opinion that Job was real—"A man in the nature of things"—Aquinas uses two texts from Scripture: Ezekiel 14:14 and James 5:11.

Summa of Theology (1894 Latin edition)

After repeating Augustine's opinion in *Enchiridion* XI, Aquinas adds, "this is part of the infinite goodness of God, that He should allow evil to exist and out of it produce good" (I, q. 2, a. 3, ad. I).

> I answer that . . . evil indicates the removal of good . . . [which] can be taken in a privative and in a negative sense . . . but the removal of good, taken in the sense of a privation, is an evil; as for instance, the privation of vision is called blindness (I, q. 48, a. 3, c).

> For evil is the absence of the good which is due to a thing by its nature . . . but evil has no formal cause, but is more a privation of form . . . a privation of order to its natural end (q. 49, a. 1, c).

> Now the order of the universe requires . . . that there are some things that can, and from time to time do, fail (art. 2, c).

> The sinking of a ship is attributed to the sailor as the cause from the fact that he has not done what is required for the safety of the ship (ad. 3).

> . . . every being as such is good that evil can exist only in good as its subject (art. 3).

PHILOSOPHERS OF RELIGION

Huston Smith (b. 1919): *The Religious Man* (1958)

Moving from Jeremiah 22:

> Thus saith the Lord . . .
> Surely I will make you a desert,
> An uninhabited city.
> I will prepare destroyers against you.

Smith states:

> The most staggering fact in the Jewish quest for meaning is the . . . meaning in suffering. . . . . there is *little* further *meaning* to be found in pain by *viewing it retrospectively as punishment for past misdoings*. If *suffering* is to be fully meaningful it must hold out . . . ways of responding to it in the present.

Question: Does Smith's interpretation contradict a view held by some in Judaism that evils are due to "sins of our fathers"?

John Hick (b. 1922): *Evil and the God of Love* (1966, 1978)

H. G. Wood Professor at the University of Birmingham, England. With regard to Prof. Hick, the distinction between "theologian" and "philosopher of religion" is, in my opinion, somewhat vague. He is in both camps.

Here I am breaking away from the philosophical focus of this book because, to be realistic, Prof. Hick is addressing an aspect of human suffering that mystifies and is of great concern to many religious people.

> 2. Theodicy versus Hell
> . . . the true nature of Christian theodicy . . . can be affirmed only by faith—it compels us to question the validity of belief in hell . . .

Hick wonders what an unending punishment in Hell can possibly achieve. He has trouble reconciling this doctrine with God's goodness or even His ability to save everyone. [This problem becomes complicated by the belief in free will and the theology of Grace, i.e., the "distribution" of God's help or aid when faced with temptations]. Protestants have usually rejected the notion of "temporal punishment" (and prayers also) after death because *The Second Book of Maccabees* is not in the Canon of their Bible. Hick then refers to the Catholic notion of Purgatory:

> Some of the Protestant theologians . . . have preferred to use instead the term progressive sanctification after death . . . our perfecting as persons."

Note: Readers might check Immanuel Kant's views on immortality for a similar teaching.

Richard Swinburne (b. 1934): *Is There a God?* (1996, Ch. 6)

Swinburne recognizes that not all deaths are necessarily evil and that in spite of the suffering in the world, many live lives of great value, pleasure, and happiness. With many others he also realizes that if free will is essential to our humanity, then possessing it opens up the risk of abuse. (Again theologians might explain evil by the non-responsiveness to God's grace.) The abuses of freedom still do not take away from the value of this magnificent gift.

(I would suggest a perusal of pages 105 to 113 wherein Swinburne addresses the notion of God as a loving parent, a notion which I referred to earlier when I questioned those who might say that love and suffering are incompatible.) Swinburne still has a problem, however, with the doctrine of Hell, a doctrine which, for him, might even call into question the very existence of God (see pp. 106-107).

> So why is there evil? Is not its existence strong evidence against the existence of God? It would be unless we can construct what is known as a theodicy, an explanation of why God would allow such evil to occur. . . . a generous God . . . will give us great responsibility for ourselves . . .

SECULAR PHILOSOPHERS

William James

American philosopher and psychologist. In his book *Pragmatism,* James tells us that if God has created the world then we are guaranteed "an ideal order that shall be permanently preserved." This order will supply "one of the deepest needs of our breast. But materialism cuts off our ultimate hopes."

In *Varieties of Religious Experience* he repeats this theme:

> God's existence is the guarantee of an ideal that shall be permanently preserved. This world may indeed . . . burn up or freeze; but if it is part of His order, the old ideals are sure to be brought to fruition, so that where God is tragedy is only provisional and partial and shipwreck and dissolution are not the absolutely final things (p. 400).

(See also William James in Chapter 3.) In another place he tells us that "Much of what we call evil is due entirely to the way men take the phenomenon. It can so often be converted into a bracing and tonic good by a simple change of the sufferer's inner attitude from one of fear to one of fight" (*Religious Experience,* p. 86).

As I mention in Chapter 3, James seems to arrive at "a God" but in his book *A Pluralistic Universe* (1986), he "defuses" the classic problem by concluding that "he is finite, either in power or in knowledge, or in both at once" (p. 311).

Another American philosopher, Edgar Brightman, also sees God as having certain limitations (see his *The Problem of God,* 1930).

Josiah Royce (1855-1916): *Studies of Good and Evil* (1896, Ch. 1)

American philosopher in the Hegelian/Fichtean idealist tradition. Royce was a professor at Harvard University from 1883 to 1916.

As with St. Thomas Aquinas, Royce finds interests as well as mystery in the sufferings ("undeserved ill") of the innocent on this earth. He recognizes the historical problem that philosophers and theologians have encountered when trying to balance the theological, purposeful structure of nature with the mechanistic laws of nature.

However, if one espouses his conception of reality, a "philosophical idealism" it would eliminate the chasms of ontological distinction between God and mankind. Job was within his rights to ask for an answer which would explain his troubles. We must realize that we are part of God's life. Our sufferings are His sufferings, our concerns are His also. Without these tragedies and evils God's life would not be perfected.

We might ask the question therefore: is this the best of all possible worlds? For God's purposes and final, eternal triumph, it would seem so.

C. S. Lewis (1898-1963): *The Problem of Pain* (1962)

In this book Lewis poses the classic "Problem of Evil" although he doesn't seem to mention God's knowledge which would also include His foreknowledge. He even poses the possibility of a finite God, as did James.

> If God were good, He would wish to make His creatures perfectly happy, and if God was almighty He would be able to do what He wished. But the creatures are not happy. . . . His omnipotence means power to do all that is intrinsically possible, not to do the intrinsically impossible.

I recommend a reading of page 24 wherein Lewis explains the consolations received from his newly found Christian faith.

CHAPTER 3

Reflections of Philosophers, Novelists, Poets, and Other Writers on Life, Death, and Immortality

As I said in the Introduction, clergy are trained professionals when it comes to their respective "revelations" and theologies. Most have studied some philosophy in college and usually some epistemology, metaphysics, ethics, and logic. Introductory courses are usually limited to a few major philosophers or the professor's favorites.

I want to cover here both major and minor (second level) philosophers. This chapter deals mainly with their thoughts on death and immortality, although in some cases I set up the discussion with some of their basic beliefs and biographical data.

Let me briefly pose and answer two questions: What is a philosopher? And why have I included novelists and poets in this chapter? I think there is general agreement that a "philosopher" is a person who is reflective, someone who "turns back" on the phenomenon of human existence and examines what many take for granted; someone who questions our ultimate origin and destiny, our place in the cosmos, as well as the cosmos itself. If philosophers tie in our destiny with the meaning of life, they will ask about the type of behavior that achieves the purpose of life—for example, what type of behavior will help everyone achieve a good, happy life? This leads philosophers into the study of the political life and law, be it civil or moral.

Many novelists, poets, and other writers reflect on human life, our hopes, our joys, and our tragedies. They write on human suffering and death. They may not be professional philosophers; they may not hold an academic rank and professorship at a university; they may have had very little or no technical philosophical education. But they are reflective; they do, as someone once said, explicate the implicit, and many have endured their own personal existential crisis.

Therefore, let us now hear from them. It is up to you, whether clergy or layperson, to cull from these writings and thoughts what you think would be most useful or applicable in the individual situation, whether it be a funeral homily, a wake, or a visit to a hospital.

THEISTIC PHILOSOPHERS

St. Augustine

Augustine was born in Tagaste, North Africa, the son of St. Monica. After a somewhat wild life and after hearing a sermon by St. Ambrose, he "converted," became a priest, a theologian, and the Bishop of Hippo in North Africa. A major work was his *Confessions*.

Naturally, Augustine believed in the immortality of the separated soul and in heaven and hell. Philosophically, he is seen as being in the Platonic "tradition." As Aquinas taught later, we will never find total fulfillment and happiness in this life. Speaking to Christ in his *Confessions*, Augustine expresses his famous words, "Our hearts are restless unless they rest in Thee O Lord."

The soul is far more important to us than the body, which (the body), if allowed to follow its natural desires unchecked by morality, could cost us our salvation.

Regarding death, evil, and suffering, Augustine writes in *The Enchiridion* that God's goodness is infinite and He would never allow evil unless He intended to bring some good out of it (see my Chapter 2).

Note: I would recommend to the reader the section on Grief in *The Confessions;* here Augustine grieves for his mother.

I would like to include a very beautiful prayer of Augustine's for people who might be in a state of discouragement for whatever reason.

God of Our Life*

God of our life, there are days when the burdens we carry chafe our shoulders and weigh us down: when the road seems dreary and endless, the skies grey and threatening; where our lives have not music in them, and our hearts are lonely, and our souls have lost their courage.

Flood the path with light, run our eyes to where the skies are full of promise, tune our hearts to brave music; give us the sense of comradeship with heroes and saints of every age; and so quicken our

spirits that we may be able to encourage the souls of all who journey
with us on the road of life, to your honor and glory.
  *(An Augustine scholar told me this is from *The Confessions*).

St. Thomas Aquinas

Roman Catholic theologian and philosopher, member of the
Dominican Order, professor at the University of Paris. Aquinas is called
the "Angelic Doctor" because of his *Treatise on the Angels*. He is highly
influential in the Catholic Church. His two main writings are the
Summa of Theology and the *Summa contra Gentiles*.

For Aquinas, of course, the ultimate end of man is supernatural, a
life, a consciousness beyond this earthly life. This is because our soul
is spiritual, "incorruptible" and thus "inexterminabilis," and therefore
immortal. (*Disputed Questions on the Soul*, q. 24; here he also quotes
St. Augustine's work *De Trinitate*).

As a Catholic theologian he believed in heaven (the presence of the
"beatific vision" forever), purgatory (a state of temporal purgation to
prepare us for the presence of God) and hell (a state of eternal
punishment). However, even though this earthly life is not our main
one, Aquinas did not see human suffering as something good in itself. In
his *Commentary on the Book of Job* he writes, "The evils which are in
this world are not to be desired for themselves, but only insofar as they
are ordered to serve good." Nevertheless, he did say in the Prologue to
this work (as mentioned in Chapter 2) that nothing is more difficult to
reconcile with divine providence than the suffering of the innocent.

In his *Summa contra Gentiles* (III, Ch. 48) Aquinas points out that
during our adult life, we cannot help but think about our approaching
death. It saddens us and we try to put it off, but our life would be happier
if we realized that this earth is not where we will find a perfect, lasting
happiness. Whatever we have gained or possessed, we will lose. No
matter how many our loved ones, we are going to be separated. This
event of death must be faced realistically. Be reconciled to it, prepare
for it, and live a happy and holy life in the time given to us by God.

Michel de Montaigne (1533-1592)

Montaigne was a lawyer and a conservative in politics and religion,
but his admiration for the Stoics and his eventual skepticism concerning the power of reason to study the soul unfortunately led him into
trouble with the official Catholic Church.

Montaigne was married and adopted a daughter. He was a classicist,
a latinist, and a sincere moral thinker who abhorred physical violence
of all kinds.

Sherwin Nuland in *How We Die* (1995), when writing of death and old age, cites Montaigne (p. 87). And Pascal in his *Pensées, 166* (1995) cites Montaigne as follows: "Not having been able to conquer death, wretchedness or ignorance, men have decided, for their own happiness, not to think about it" (i, 20).

Montaigne's famous essay on this subject is "To Philosophize Is to Learn to Die" (1987). Why do people die? "Give place to others, as others have given place to you." "Your death is part of the order of the universe, 'tis a part of the world . . . 'tis the condition of your creation: (pp. 103-104). Before our death we should give some thought to its inevitable reality, its imminence. We all await death: be resigned, reconciled, "wait patiently and tranquilly."

> The utility of living consists not in the length of days, but in the use of time; a man may have lived long, yet lived a little (p. 106).

Blaise Pascal (1623-1662)

French mathematician and physicist. Pascal had religious doubts but experienced a "conversion," after which he sewed a "memorial" into his jacket which read: "Certitude . . . joy . . . God of Jesus Christ . . . Let me never be separated from Him." Until then he had been very pessimistic about his chances for salvation.

Pascal agreed with Ovid: "Call no man happy until he is dead." For Pascal "eternal happiness begins at death." (All quotations here are from his main work, *Pensées,* 1670/1995). He believed in the immortality of the soul, but his concepts of Christ's mercy and heaven seem confused. He seemed to commit the fallacy of bifurcation: "either an eternity of suffering, or eternal nothingness." Death is a "constant threat," but at least it will put an end to the "vicissitudes in this life." People should devote their lives and efforts to pleasing God or searching for Him—not to any human and certainly not to Pascal, "because I am no one's ultimate end, and cannot satisfy them. Am I not (myself) near death. So the object of their attachment will die" (Pensées, 15).

> Man is not worthy of God, but he is not incapable of being made worthy of Him (Pensées, 271).

> Distraction: It is easier to put up with death without thinking about it, than with the idea of death when there is no danger of it (Pensées, 170).

Immanuel Kant (1724-1804)

Famous German philosopher. Kant was born in the former Königsburg. Although he is usually seen as an "adversary" by scholastic philosophers, it seems that in the final analysis (his *Critique of Practical Reason*, 1788/1949) he comes round to the possibility of "reasoning" to God, freedom, and human immortality.

If we are obliged to obey the moral law, says Kant, we must possess free will. However, because of our weak human nature and moral failures we can never attain perfect virtue and holiness in a single lifetime. Life must, therefore, continue in order to fulfill this natural desire for holiness. This is a "postulate" of our Practical Reason.

Arthur Schopenhauer (1788-1860)

German philosopher. Schopenhauer's main writing, *The World as Will and Idea* (1818 original [Engl. tr. 1883]), exhibits a broad spectrum of interests and knowledge: metaphysics, aesthetics, theology, and so forth. Until I read this book, I had only a "nodding" acquaintance with him and his general characterization as a pessimist.

Schopenhauer rejects the Stoic desire for a life without suffering, the hope of a "blessed life," tranquil and serene. Such a life, he believes, is very unrealistic. Instead of suicide following trials and tribulations, he recommends the example "Of the holy man of Christianity who stands before us in perfect virtue, holiness, and sublimity, yet in a state of supreme suffering" (*World as Idea*, Bk. I, p. 120). In his *Metaphysics of Love and the Sexes* (1928) Schopenhauer refers to the suffering Jesus as "The Saviour." (Several Gospel quotations are to be found in his writings.)

On life and death he writes:

> Every breath we draw wards off the death that is constantly intruding upon us . . . through every meal we eat, every sleep we take. . . . In the end death must conquer for we become subject to him through birth, and he only plays for a little while with his prey before he swallows it up (1928 Modern Library Edition).

Unfortunately, Schopenhauer feels that the "unspeakable suffering" of humanity makes a "bitter mockery" even of Christian optimism.

I once read that he opined that "immortality would be the perpetuation of a great mistake," yet when speaking of suicide he tells us, "It affords us no escape" because everyone must continue to be. He tells us that "the suicide really wills life but is only dissatisfied with the conditions under which it is presented to him," meaning, of course, human suffering.

I will end with a view of Schopenhauer's that I find a bit strange, with echoes of Epictetus: Schopenhauer can't figure out why some people worry about a future eternity without being when they don't seem to be bothered emotionally about the eternity behind them.

Although he speaks of Jesus as our "Saviour," I still do not find his writing absolutely clear on the possibility of our immortality. Perhaps in German his opinions would be clearer. In the end, of course, they would be only that: his opinions.

Fyodor Dostoevsky (1821-1881)

Russian novelist. Dostoevsky presented his philosophy through literature. He was a member of the Russian military for a short while, but owing to political activities, he was sent to Siberia for ten years, a stay that aggravated an epileptic condition.

The death of his wife of seven years, mounting debt, and loneliness are said to account for the pessimistic views expressed in some of his writings. He died in St. Petersburg of a brain hemorrhage.

To get on top of this man's thought, I recommend a reading of *The Brothers Karamazov*. Are we controlled by our intellects, reason, and law, or by sheer free will? Freedom ends up as a self-destructive position. This is the position of the "Grand Inquisitor." On the other hand, there is the freedom that comes with immersion in the Christian faith. When one chooses Christ, *death* has a meaning—personal immortality; but when we choose Christ, we cannot have absolute, unlimited freedom of action. Dostoevsky returns to his Russian Orthodox faith and moral law, but each of us must *freely* seek our happiness and salvation within the constraints of Christ's freedom.

Dostoevsky's words "We are citizens of eternity" are quoted (p. 149) by Norman Vincent Peale in *Faith is the Answer* (1982). And "Believe that God loves you in a way you cannot imagine" is quoted by Jacques Maritain in *Challenges and Renewals* (1966).

Charles Sanders Peirce

Professor of Philosophy at Harvard and Johns Hopkins Universities. Peirce is considered one of the greatest American philosophers and modern logicians. However, good fortune did not seem to smile on him throughout most of his life, owing to personality problems, career problems, and disease. His final years ended in poverty, discomfort, and death from cancer.

How could he endure all this? Commentators on Peirce seem to be agreed that he believed in the "reality" of God, a term he preferred to "exist" because as he saw it, to "exist" is to interact with other "like things."

Peirce had a "nest" of "arguments" for the reality of God (6.435) (6.457) (6.479) in which he used terms like "Humble," "Neglected" and "Musement." He believed that we can have positive knowledge of God and should reject a totally "negative theology." Nevertheless, we must recognize the importance of "vagueness." He wrote about this to James (8.262), pointing out that God is not finite even though our knowledge of Him is not precise.

To me this means that while God may be loving, merciful and just, we do not perfectly understand these virtues when predicated of Him.

I believe he once referred to Christ as "the Master." I hope his faith was of some consolation during the final, difficult days, which preceded his death from cancer. (All references are from the Volumes and Paragraphs of the Hartshorne *Collected Works.*)

Note: The realization that many highly intelligent people (intellectuals) are atheists or agnostics disturbs some theists. These "believers" can take consolation in the fact that Peirce, surely of an intellectual capacity equal to that of many an atheist, shared their faith.

William James

James was born into a wealthy American family. His brother, Henry James, was a famous writer. William was born in New York City; his early education was what some might call "cosmopolitan." At Harvard he studied medicine and psychology, and he eventually wrote in the field of psychology. He studied under Peirce and adapted a version of Peirce's Pragmatism (or Pragmaticism). William James's major works are *Pragmatism and Four Essays on Truth* (1907) and *The Varieties of Religious Experience* (1901).

James had several psychological problems of his own, including the question of free will. He had "witnessed" two great evils and causes of human suffering: slavery and the Civil War. In *The Varieties of Religious Experience* he wrote:

> God is the natural appellation, for *us Christians* at least for the supreme reality. . . . We and God have business with each other and [by] opening ourselves to his influence, our deepest destiny is fulfilled. God's existence is the guarantee of an ideal order . . . *so that where God is, tragedy is only provisional* and partial and shipwreck and dissolution are not the absolutely final things (p. 400; emphasis in original).

Note: One dictionary definition of provisional is "temporary."

James knew well the "sectarian scientific attitude" of his day, but declared the belief in empirical data only to be "humbug" (*Varieties,* p. 401).

Hastings Rashdall (1858-1924)

English theologian, philosopher, and historian Rashdall was born in London. He studied at Oxford and was a fellow at Herford College and Chaplain and Divinity tutor at Balliol College. Philosophically, he was a "personal idealist": "Only if we suppose that the present life . . . has an end which lies beyond the limits of the present natural order . . . can we find a rational meaning of human life" (from his major work, *The Theory of Good and Evil,* 1907).

Martin Buber (1878-1965)

Professor at Hebrew University, Jerusalem. Buber was born in Vienna and left Europe for Palestine in 1938.

For Buber, God was not some nonpersonal God of the philosophers, but rather a personal God, one with whom we can communicate and perhaps even dialogue—He is our "thou" and we are His "thou." The bible is the story of human communication with God. When suffering seems unbearable, the time has come to open up this dialogue—even if we have never done so before (from the *Encyclopedia of Philosophy,* Vol. I, 1967).

Karl Jaspers (1883-1969)

German psychologist and existential philosopher. Jaspers was born in Oldburg. He was a Christian in his own way. We must discover the inner vitality of Christianity, says Jaspers, which might demand compromise with immutable doctrines if not the institutional churches. However, we cannot dispense with the Bible. If we restrict our knowledge and reality to what comes from empirical evidence, we can end up rejecting God and could have difficulty explaining the uniqueness of our special kind of being (our humanness).

Jaspers does not offer us much consolation. He fears annihilation; he wonders whether the afterlife might only be "temporary." He gets no help from a Protestantism fraught with fanaticism, or Catholicism, which is too totalitarian (or course, for Jaspers, freedom is a major element of our humanity).

He espouses an intellectual agnosticism about a personal God because human concepts and language fall short when faced with the trans-cendence of "Being-Itself." Rather than immersing ourselves in the physical and aesthetic delights of this world in order to avoid facing the reality of our finitude, we should simply live authentically and humanly, exercising our actuality as free beings, being self-creative. We should have a "philosophical faith" mixed with those biblical passages that might help us overcome our "forlornness."

Jacques Maritain (1881-1973)

Held the Chair of Thomistic Philosophy at Princeton University, Maritain was born in Paris and studied at the Sorbonne, Heidelburg, and the Pontifical Institute of Medieval Studies. A former Aristotelian-Thomist, he converted to Catholicism in 1906. One of his main writings is *Challenges and Renewals* (1966). On the "human condition," Maritain tells us that the "spirit is immortal, and matter imposes the law of death on the body animated by it" (p. 371). Our destiny, our telos, is to seek a *good moral life* once we realize its possibility and importance; but without our consciously realizing it, this is actually a natural desire for the absolute good, God—and we seek this good for its own sake.

Again, on the human condition Maritain quotes Mircea Eliade (a specialist in comparative religion) from his *The Myth of Eternal Return* (1954):

> The acceptance of time and of history—far from being matter of course for man—is a difficult and dearly paid achievement. *Man is naturally frightened* by *the irreversibility of his own duration* [emphasis in original].

Maritain wonders at times whether Ovid was right: it might have been better, at least for some, if they had never been born. (However, I don't think this was Maritain's definitive view of life.)

Gabriel Marcel (1889-1973)

Catholic French existential philosopher playwright and drama critic. Marcel was born in Paris. His father was an agnostic; his aunt, who helped raise him, was Protestant (his mother died when he was only four years old). He converted to Catholicism in 1929 at age forty-six.

Marcel's drama *The Broken World* (1933) portrayed the problems of the superficiality of human relationships in the twentieth century.

For clergy or speakers who want to get profoundly philosophical, I would recommend Marcel's *Philosophy of Existence* (1948), especially the section "The Ontological Mystery." Marcel distinguishes between memories of the dead who were mere acquaintances or even relatives and memories of those who were very significant to us. These latter have been "granted to [us] as a presence," and we must remain *open* to their presence. The memory of someone in the first category he calls an "effigy." Marcel speaks of a "fidelity" to the deceased that is "creative," a "presence" that is a "reality," a "kind of influx," and it is important for us to be "permeable" to this influx. Creative fidelity consists in maintaining ourselves actively in a "permeable state." If one consults *Philosophy of Existence,* it would be useful to examine the reflections preceding and following these thoughts; also, to see his relationship to Martin Buber who speaks of our special response to God's presence.

Constantly a witness to the pessimistic philosophies of Camus and Sartre, Marcel developed an existential theory (a metaphysic) of hope, namely, that we do have a social destiny given by our Creator. True, we must live with many fears and desires, but we are not the total, sole creator of values and our own essence. Sartre thought that all love is doomed to failure, but Marcel saw the reciprocal love of giving for and to each other as our imaging the Holy Trinity. I assume that here he means the relations of the three Persons to each other.

ATHEISTIC/AGNOSTIC PHILOSOPHERS

Friedrich Nietzsche (1844-1900)

German philosopher. Nietzsche was a student of classical studies at the University of Leipzig, then professor of philosophy at Basel until 1879. Following an illness contracted during the Franco-Prussian War while working as a medical orderly, his health gradually deteriorated after 1879.

Note: I think we should be careful about personal attacks or absolute statements on the man or his views on God and Christianity. His views are very nuanced, if not vague.

Anyone wishing to explore Nietzsche's thought should ponder the difference between his dislike of Christianity and an authentic atheistic position. His famous "God is dead" statement from *Thus Spake Zarathustra* (1927/54) might only be an indictment of the modern Europeans who "killed" Him by their secularism, materialism, and indifference.

I think much of the essence of Nietzsche's thought is in his book *Ecce Homo* (1927/54). In his famous "transvaluation of all values," all Christian values or virtues become vices (e.g., helping the weak of the world) and what are considered vices (e.g., rule by the strong) become virtues. In a section titled "Why I Am So Clever," he tells us:

> God; the "immortality of the soul," "salvation," a "beyond"—these are mere notions to which I paid no attention, on which I never wasted my time. . . . I am quite unacquainted with atheism as a result. . . . I am too inquisitive, too skeptical, too arrogant to let

myself be satisfied with an obvious and crass solution of theories. God is such an obvious and crass solution. . . . He is nothing but a coarse commandment against us: Ye shall not think (p. 834).

He then tells us that for him to believe in Christianity would be an absurdity.

On death itself he writes, "The *superior man* should not be taken unawares, by ambush. Be waiting, aware, joyfully and proudly assuming death as the natural termination of life" (p. 835; emphasis in original).

Note: We see Christianity taking some heavy blows here. Humanity is certainly not Nietzsche's forte. He says he hasn't paid attention to God and God's authority bothers him, but these are not necessarily assertions of the nonexistence of God. Since I have not read his entire corpus, I leave it at that.

Sigmund Freud (1856-1939)

Viennese psychoanalyst. Freud died a painful death from cancer, after fleeing to England in 1938. He was antipathetic to religion and to any consolations it might give us. In his thinking, an inherent danger of religion is that it extends our childish immaturity. Subconsciously we are seeking the protraction of dependence on a heavenly "father." In order to solve human problems and to conquer diseases, religious people resort to prayer and hope for miracles. This is bad because it distracts us from the hard scientific work needed to attain answers and solutions. How to deal with the final moments: "We should create a platonic romance with death" (from *Thoughts for the Times on War and Death,* 1915).

Albert Camus (1931-1960)

French existentialist philosopher and novelist. Camus' philosophy came through his novels, including *The Stranger* and *The Plague,* and his essays, such as "The Myth of Sisyphus." Camus was a French Algerian whose existential crisis was the Algerian civil war (French Foreign Legion vs. Algerian rebels), an extremely vicious war.

As is the case with most philosophers on whom non-existentialists bestow the appellation "existentialist," Camus deals with various "themes" (e.g., absurdity, evil, freedom), not philosophical doctrines. Camus has usually been considered an atheist, but I have heard that toward the end of his life (he died of a car accident in Paris), he was engaging Dominicans in debate on the existence of God. Was he searching?

The presence of evil and suffering in the world profoundly disturbed him. His problem with religious faith caused him, unlike William James, to see no rational explanation for suffering. Life itself became pointless, without purpose, futile. No goal becomes better than any other, or, if it is better, there is no way of knowing it. In "The Myth of Sisyphus" he speaks of "the insane character of daily obligation and the uselessness of suffering." He felt like a stranger in an alien world: "The divorce between man and his life, the actor and his setting, is properly called the feeling of absurdity."

Bertrand Russell (1872-1970)

British philosopher and mathematician. Russell graduated from Cambridge University in 1894. During World War I he was dismissed from his professorship at Cambridge because of his pacifist views. Perhaps it was his pacifism that led him to appreciate the message and person of Jesus Christ, although he felt that Christians had rarely lived up to the teachings of the founder of their religion.

During a television interview, he said he was not *certain* that there is no God, but thought it *improbable*. He sometimes saw himself more as an agnostic than an atheist. Religion, with its doctrine of hell, just upsets people by causing great fear. There cannot be a hell if there is no immortality, and he thought it more probable that the brain, or physical energy, is the "mind" rather than a spiritual soul. On the other hand, in his middle years he did think the findings of psychic research should be given tolerant consideration.

Martin Heidegger (1889-1976)

German philosopher, metaphysician. Heidegger's writing, as in *Introduction to Metaphysics* (1953), is not devoid of existential themes. He was born in Germany's Black Forest, a region to which he retreated in his twilight years. He was professor and rector of the University of Freiburg. His ties with the Nazi party in 1933 hurt his career after World War II.

In another famous work, *Being and Time* (1962), Heidegger defines us: "Man is a being unto death." After leaving a Jesuit seminary he adopted a negative attitude toward religion and moved toward an atheistic position. He came to the conclusion that our race is *not* the effect of a transcendent Creator and therefore there is no racial essence. *We* create ourselves throughout the course of our life. We are simply here, on the scene, facing death. This is our "being-there," our "dasein" (note the similarity to Sartre).

As Nietzsche pointed out in his *Joyful Wisdom* (1881/1960), we have eliminated God from our lives. Heidegger agrees—but this leaves an emptiness in our lives. We have nothing to fall back on. As William James wondered: how can we explain tragedies? Suffering? All living things will die, but we humans *know* we are going to die. Therefore, says Heidegger, cultivate the awareness of death. Don't cut out the consciousness of death. Death gives a sense of urgency to life because it is a purely individual act. No one can do it for us. At death our existence is completed. We have come from nothing and will return to nothing. It is our vocation to realize this.

Although Heidegger has serious problems with the God and "God talk" of the Christian theology, he still maintains that the way to transcend meaninglessness and death is to outwit them. Don't get so attached to the things and events and people of this world that the fear of death overwhelms you. Don't be ambushed by it. (Are we hearing echoes here of his early Jesuit spiritual reflections?) I often wonder if this attitude toward and love of *solitude,* which Heidegger exhibited in his life, was simply his way of preparing for the grave.

Jean-Paul Sartre (1889-1980)

French existentialist philosopher. Sartre trained at the Sorbonne. Two of his most famous works are *Being and Nothingness* (1956) and *Existentialism Is a Humanism* (1947).

With Sartre we have what might be termed a "problem of reconciliation." If an all-powerful, ubiquitous God controls all Being by his conserving power and therefore presence to His creation, how can a person's internal act of the will be free? We can't have it both ways. Sartre opts for freedom—therefore, no God. This means that while we are here "on the scene," as a race we have no purpose, no raison d'être, no ultimate destiny except the grave. Why? Because we have no creator. Intelligent efficient causes act intentionally, purposefully. Therefore, it falls to individuals to create their own "essence" by their choices (choix) or decisions. (Thus existence precedes essence.) Unfortunately, for Sartre, man "is a useless passion."

Many of our choices are critical to our earthly happiness, thus creating great anguish (angoisse) throughout our life—which is the *only* life we will ever have. Since there is no God to preserve our consciousness, there is no personal immortality. Anyway, God's love for us would only turn us into objects and destroy our subjectivity. All love is doomed to failure.

Sartre agrees with Heidegger, Lamont, Nietzsche, and Freud that our awareness of death should be cultivated and prepared for while at the same time we live life to the fullest.

Corliss Lamont (1902-1995)

Humanistic philosopher, political activist, and educator. Lamont studied at Harvard and Oxford (graduate studies) and was a professor at Columbia University. (1928 to 1932 and 1947 to 1959). He was once subpoenaed by Senator Joseph McCarthy; he was at one time director of the American Civil Liberties Union. Lamont wrote *The Philosophy of Humanism* (1957) and an article for *The Humanist* titled "The Crisis Called Death" (1967). As a secular humanist he cannot believe in a life after death but he is not happy about his future oblivion.

> The humanist faces his own death and that of others with more equanimity than the average person because he realizes that in the process of Nature death is a necessary corollary of life (Vol. 27, p. 19).

> I would like to go on living indefinitely (Vol. 27, p. 19).

> Our main antidote for death is preoccupation with life (Vol. 27, p. 19).

PAGAN PHILOSOPHERS

Socrates (469-399 B.C.) and Plato

Most of what we know about Socrates we get from Plato's *Dialogues*. Scholars see few differences between the thoughts of these two men, especially in Plato's early writings. From these two Pagan philosophers we have the following:

1. The human soul exists and is immortal (*Phaedo*).
2. Perhaps the gods have prepared a wonderful dwelling "place" for the just (*Crito*).
3. Death is not to be feared nor should we mourn excessively. Only the body has died, not the real person (*Crito*).
4. We should be excited about meeting famous personages who have gone before us (perhaps even relatives) (*The Apology*).
5. Therefore, the "goods" of the soul are superior to those of the body. In fact, evil people will probably have to suffer until forgiven by those they have offended (*Crito*).

These beliefs explain why, in early Christianity, many intellectuals (Augustine and others) held philosophical views sometimes termed "neo-Platonic."

Epicurus (341-270 B.C.)

Epicurus was from the island of Samos. He knew followers of Plato and Democritus. He founded an Epicurean community (The Garden) at Athens in 307-306 B.C.

While I cannot agree with his rather cavalier dismissal of the "anticipation" of death bothering us, I must admit he gives us an interesting line of reasoning. Schopenhauer quoted one of Epicurus's favorite maxims in his *World as Will and Idea* (1818): "Would you learn how to pass your years tranquilly; do not let greedy desire vex and agitate you." The famed Stoic tranquility required freedom from fear—the fear of death being the worst.

In a "Letter to Menoeceus," Epicurus attempts to console us:

> Become accustomed to the belief that death is nothing to us. For all good and evil consists in sensation, but death is deprivation of sensation. And mortality of life enjoyable, not because it adds to it an infinite span of time, but because it takes away the craving for immortality. For there is nothing terrible in life for the man who has truly comprehended that there is nothing terrible in not living. So that man speaks but idly who says that he fears death not because it will be painful when it comes, but because it is painful in anticipation. For that which gives no trouble when it comes, is but an empty pain in anticipation. So death, the most terrifying of ills, is nothing to us, since so long as we exist death is not with us; but when death comes, then we do not exist. It does not then concern either the living or the dead, since for the former it is not, and the latter are no more.
>
> But the many at one moment shun death as the greatest of evils, at another yearn for it as a respite from the evils of life. But the wise man neither seeks to escape life nor fears the cessation of life, for neither does life offend him nor does the absence of life seem to be any evil. And just as with food he does not seek simply the larger share and nothing else, but rather the most pleasant, so he seeks to enjoy not the longest period of time, but the most pleasant.

Marcus Tullius Cicero (106-43 B.C.)

Roman lawyer, orator, and Stoic philosopher. (On stoicism, see the paragraph below on Marcus Aurelius.) In his book *On the Commonwealth,* Cicero speaks of a natural moral law—"True Law," "which is right reason according to our nature." God is its author and enforcer. (I imagine that by "God"—Deus—he means the Logos.)

From Cicero's *Tusculan Disputations:*

> For we are not born or created idly or fortuitously; but doubtless there is some power which takes some thought for the race of men,

and which was not likely to create and foster what—where it had accomplished all its toils—would sink into everlasting misery and death (*Disputation I*, XLIX, p. 143).

Here we see Cicero sharing the belief (or hope) of many Christians that a God of infinite love and intelligence would never sentence His human creations to everlasting punishment.

Epictetus (c.50-c.130)

Stoic philosopher. Epictetus was a highly moral Stoic thinker and believer in the Stoic conception of God. He rose above a background of slavery and exile. While professing the Stoic apathy/tranquility, he also encouraged personal responsibility for our actions. Nevertheless, in good Stoic fashion, he taught the existence of a cosmic force, a "fate" that controls a great many events in the universe, including the ultimate destiny of each human being. Our death, then, is an event we may as well accept.

Some famous sayings (from *):

> I cannot escape death, but can I not escape the dread of it.

> Demand not that events should happen as you wish; but, wish them to happen as they do happen and you will do well.

*Cited by Theodore Denise and Sheldon Peterfreund in *Great Traditions in Ethics,* 7th ed., Wadsworth, Belmont, California, 1992, p. 77.

Marcus Aurelius (121-180)

Roman Emperor and Stoic philosopher. According to Marcus Aurelius, fate (Logos?) allows us a certain amount of time and no more. We must keep in mind that Stoicism taught resignation, a stoic "apathy" to whatever fate sends us. Although we cannot control many predestined events, we can at least control our attitude toward them. After death we will be with the gods. As with birth, death is simply one of Nature's secrets. At death, then, we depart for a "far shore." Hopefully, the gods will be there to receive us and to eliminate all pain. If not, we go into nothingness. However, Aurelius does seem to have believed that the good Stoic will be welcomed into the gods' domain.

Chief Seattle (c.1790-1866)

The pioneers of Seattle named their city for Chief Sealth, a Duwamish Indian who befriended them (*World Book Encyclopedia,* Vol. 17). He is quoted in DeSpelder and Strickland's *The Last Dance* (1996):

To us the ashes of our ancestors are sacred and their resting place is hallowed ground. . . . Be just and deal kindly with my people, for the dead are not powerless. Dead, did I say? There is no death, only a change of worlds.

NOVELISTS, POETS, AND OTHER WRITERS

William Cullen Bryant (1794-1878)

American poet and newspaper editor (New York *Evening Post*). Bryant was born in Cummington, Massachusetts. Having rejected the Calvinism of his parents, he espoused Unitarianism; he took an anti-slavery stance.

His most famous poem, "Thanatopsis," was inspired by his reading of the English "Graveyard" poets. The poem was submitted by his father to the *North American Review* in 1818. The final section was added when Bryant was twenty-nine years of age. What follows is the end of the first section and the final section (emphasis in original):

> *Take note of thy departure? All that breathe*
> *Will share thy destiny.*
>
> The youth in life's green spring, and he who goes
> In full strength of years, matron, and maid,
> And the sweet babe, and the grey-headed man
> Shall one by one be gathered to thy side.
> By those, who in their turn shall follow them.
>
> *So live, that* when thy summons comes to join
> *The innumerable caravan,* which moves
> To *that mysterious* realm, where each shall take
> His chamber in the silent halls of death,
> *Thou go not, like the quarry-slave at night.*

Note: Compare this with Nietzsche and Heidegger.

Emily Dickinson (1830-1886)

American transcendentalist poet. Dickinson was born in Amherst, Massachusetts. She is considered influential on twentieth century poets.

Dickinson had various sorrows in her life. Her father died when she was forty-four. What one might call her "love life" did not work out well, and the carnage of the Civil War disturbed her greatly.

Note: Scholarly citation of Dickinson's poems and letters is not an easy task. There have been several anthologies in which some are titled, others are identified by the first line, and others identified by a number. I will give these as I have found them and simply suggest that the reader might consult an anthology or an American literature professor.

A very famous poem "The Chariot," or simply #712. The first stanza follows:

The Chariot

Because I could not stop for death—
He kindly stopped for me—
The Carriage held but just Ourselves—
And Immortality.

The next poem is given in its entirety.

The Battlefield

They dropped like flakes, they dropped like stars,
    Like petals from a rose,
When suddenly across the June
    A wind with fingers goes.

They perished in the seamless grass—
    No eye could find the place;
But God on his repealless list
    Can summon every face.

Note: This poem can easily be linked to the deaths of the Ketcham brothers in the Civil War in the section "Death of a Sibling" in Chapter 4.

I have read of a poem (#45) the first line of which reads, "There's something quieter than sleep," but I have not been able to find it. It seems to deal with suggestive imagery of the dead body and the conventions of mourning.

Several more of Dickinson's poems:

Parting

My life closed twice before its close;
    It yet remains to see
If immortality unveil
    A third event to me,

So huge, so hopeless to conceive,
    As these that twice befall.
Parting is all we know of heaven,
    And all we need of hell.

Dying

I heard a fly buzz when I died;
   The stillness round my form
Was like the stillness in the air
   Between the heaves of storm.

The eyes beside had wrung them dry,
   And breaths were gathering sure
For that last onset, when the king
   Be witnessed in his power.

I willed my keepsakes, signed away
   What portion of me I
Could make assignable,—and then
   There interposed a fly,

With blue, uncertain, stumbling buzz,
   Between the light and me;
And then the windows failed, and then
   I could not see to see.

Immortality

It is an honorable thought,
   And makes one lift one's hat,
As one encountered gentlefolk
   Upon a daily street,
That we've immortal place,
   Though pyramids decay,
And kingdoms, like the orchard,
   Flit resettle away.

XXXI

Death is a dialogue between
The spirit and the dust
"Dissolve," says Death, the spirit, "Sir,"
I have another trust.

John Donne (1573-1631)

Anglican clergyman and Dean of St. Paul's church in London. Donne was educated at Oxford and Cambridge. Originally a Catholic, he entered the Anglican church in 1615. He is considered one of the first of England's "metaphysical poets."

Donne was Hemingway's source for the well known lines, "No man is an island, entire of itself; every man is a piece of the continent, a part of the main. Never send to know for whom the bell tolls; it tolls for thee" (see below on Hemingway).

One of Donne's more famous poems:

Death, Be Not Proud

Death, be not proud, though some have called thee
Mighty and dreadful, for thou are not so;
For those whom thou think'st thou dost overthrow
Die not, poor Death; nor yet canst thou kill me.
From rest and sleep, which but thy picture be,
Much pleasure; then from thee much more must flow;
And soonest our best men with thee do go—
Rest of their bones and souls' delivery!
Thou'rt slave to fate, chance, kings, and desperate men,
And dost with poison, war, and sickness dwell;
And poppy or charms can make us sleep well
And better than thy stroke. Why swell'st thou then?
One short sleep passed, we wake eternally,
And Death shall be no more; Death, thou shalt die.

Viktor Frankl (1905-1997)

Psychoanalyst and author. Frankl was born in Vienna and received his M.D. from the city's university. He studied psychoanalysis under Adler and taught neurology and psychiatry at the university. His career ended when he was arrested by the Nazis in 1942. His wife and parents were killed. Frankl survived three years in Auschwitz and Dachau.

After the war, he wrote of his death camp experiences and developed his theory of "Logotherapy," brought out in his famous book *Man's Search for Meaning* (1959). Most of what I describe here is from that book.

Frankl tells us that although many survived the Nazi death camps in body, their spirits were shattered and "dead." But Frankl never lost hope. He quotes Nietzsche: "He who has a 'why' to live for can bear almost any 'how.'" A man "may retain his human dignity" if he himself can decide what shall become of him. On this thought, he quotes Dostoevskys: *"There is only one thing that I dread: not to be worthy of my suffering."*

Frankl wrote in *Man's Search for Meaning* that many who suffered and died in the camps

> bore witness that the last inner freedom cannot be lost . . . the way they bore their suffering was a genuine inner achievement. It . . . makes life meaningful and purposeful. . . .

If there is meaning to life at all, then there must be meaning in suffering (pp. 66-67).

Resorting to the Stoic attitude toward life, he tells us that "The way in which a man accepts his fate . . . even under the most difficult circumstances" adds a "deeper meaning to his life" (p. 67).

Ernest Hemingway (1899-1961)

Nobel Prize-winning American novelist. Hemingway wrote *The Old Man and the Sea, A Farewell to Arms, The Sun Also Rises,* and *For Whom the Bell Tolls,* among other novels and stories. Although wounded in World War I in Italy (as an ambulance driver), he proceeded to live an exciting life, but died by his own hand July 21, 1961. He was known to have dwelled on the violent nature of man.

Hemingway, very upset and grieving because of the recent death from cancer of his close friend Gary Cooper, committed suicide. (Cooper had found some consolation from his new Catholic faith while Hemingway referred to himself as a "failed Catholic.")

According to his good friend and biographer A. E. Hotchner, Hemmingway felt that since he couldn't write anymore (in his own opinion) he might as well "retire" while at the top of his game, as did DiMaggio, Williams, and Marciano—but he added—"how does a writer retire? No one accepts that his legs are shot, etc."

Interestingly enough, Hotchner later lit a candle in the Dominican Church of Santa Maria Sopra Minerva in Rome because as he remarked, it was "his church." Ernest Hemingway, a tortured soul, who, I believe, found his final peace with God.

When asked by a German journalist: "Herr Hemingway, can you sum up your feelings about death?" he answered: "Yes, just another whore" (from *Papa Hemingway,* by A. E. Hotchner (1966), pp. 290, 298, 303-304).

Eugene Ionesco (1912-1994)

Playwright, famed for his part in the "Theatre of the Absurd." Ionesco spent most of his life in France. His works deal with the tragicomic nature of modern Western culture and the unquestioning acceptance of European values. He thought the only kind of play that mirrors the mechanical (i.e., unthinking, noncritical) nature of modern civilization and the futility of human actions *is* the *Absurd,* the anti-real. Excellent examples are *Les Chaises* (The Chairs) and *The Fragments of a Journal.* From *Fragments* (1968):

> I cannot understand how we humans, for hundreds of years, have accepted an existence haunted by the fear of death. . . . How can mankind have put up with being here, having been *flung* here, with *no explanation. . . . All philosophies,* all sciences have proved unable *to provide a key to the mystery*[1] (p. 31; emphasis in original).

We've been "conditioned, dragged on a leash," victims of a great "hoax." In other sections of his *Fragments* he expresses an existential "forlornness." I would recommend readers also examine other parts of this book.

Omar Khayyam (c.1050-c.1123)

Persian poet, mathematician, astronomer. Omar Khayyam born in Naishapur in Khorassan, Persia. His most famous work is probably the *Rubaiyat* (Quatrains). The translation used here is by Edward Fitzgerald (1899). Fitzgerald opined that Omar Khayyam was something of a philosopher as well as a poet. Certain quatrains are very well known, especially those that show a hedonistic bent (Epicurean?), although I think Fitzgerald perceived a sufi mysticism to be present at times.

Two lesser-known quatrains follow, which I think are more relevant to our subject and therefore might be more useful to readers.

> Oh threats of Hell and Hopes of Paradise
> One thing at least is certain—*This* life flies;
> One thing is certain and the rest is lies;
> The Flower that once has blown forever dies (LXIII).

> Strange is it not? that of the myriads who
> Before us pass'd the door of darkness through,
> Not one returns to tell us of the Road,
> Which to discover we must travel too (LXIV).

And the famous quatrain:

> The moving finger writes; and having writ,
> Moves on: nor all your Piety nor Wit
> Shall lure it back to cancel half a line,
> Nor all your tears wash not a word of it (LXXI).

Note: Unlike motion, the poet is saying, time moves only inexorably forward.

---

[1] I beg to differ. Many philosophies and religions have provided us with "explanations" and answers to life's mysteries. Because we do not have the whole truth or all the answers doesn't mean we haven't attained some.

Elisabeth Kübler-Ross (b. 1926)

Even before attending medical school, Kübler-Ross gave medical assistance to the people of war-torn Poland, and probably even Germany. While at medical school in Switzerland, she met and married a fellow student, an American, and came to the United States to practice. The plight of terminally ill patients caused her to become involved in death and dying workshops and led to the writing of nine books on the subject. Her latest book, and I think she believes it to be her final one, is *The Wheel of Life* (1997). I recommend this book, along with *Questions and Answers on Death and Dying* (1974).

As you may know, Dr. Kübler-Ross won some fame for her five steps of response to the news that one is terminally ill: denial, anger, bargaining with God, depression, and acceptance (see *On Death and Dying*, 1969). However, *she* does not believe that people should be told absolutely that they are dying. Hope should always be held out to them.

Going back to a problem I referred to in my Introduction, Kübler-Ross relates the story of some seminarians from the Chicago Theological Seminary who approached her with a request for lectures. They were familiar with the Bible but had no experience with dying people, nor had they ever been at a deathbed—exemplifying the problem that clergy sometimes experience in such situations. Another time, at the end of a session with a dying person, a priest admitted to Kübler-Ross, "I don't know what to say, so I don't say anything." She concluded that even clergy sometimes need counsel in this situation.

Because of her strong belief in human immortality, Kübler-Ross feels that "dying is nothing to fear." Depending on how you have lived your life, it can be one of the great experiences of life itself. It is merely a transition to another and better state of existence. It struck her that many medical students had what we call "existential grief" (see Chapter 4), a fear of their own death. We know that many doctors who "lose" a patient see death as a "defeat." Kübler-Ross feels that God determines this, not the doctor. She feels that a life ends "when you have learned everything you are supposed to learn." She tells of her own mother, the ultimate self-sufficient person, who ended her days in a nursing home utterly dependent on others. "What lesson was God trying to teach her?" asks Kübler-Ross. Maybe that sometimes we must lean on others; this is a good lesson for us as well.

How much can we "handle"? If we have faith in God and ourselves we can acquiesce to pain and suffering. Kübler-Ross was especially struck by the drawings of butterflies on the barracks walls of a Nazi death camp (Majdanek). Why butterflies? Then it came to her: these people—

men, women, and children—would soon leave the "cocoon" of their bodies and that hellish place and move to freedom and peace.

> Some forever bloom for only a few days—everybody admires them as a sign of spring and hope. Then they die—but they have done what they needed to do (*Wheel of Life*, p. 227).

Kübler-Ross believes in ghosts and near death experiences and says that those who have had such experiences fear death no longer. She discusses a message from her dead husband (*Wheel of Life*, pp. 271-273). Finally, for herself, she thinks her "death will come to me like a warm embrace"; that this life represents only a brief span of our total existence.

> When we have passed the tests we were sent to Earth to learn, we are allowed to graduate. We are allowed to shed our body, which imprisons our soul the way a cocoon encloses the *future butterfly,* and when the time is right we can let go of it. Then we will be free of pain, free of fears and free of worries . . . free as a beautiful butterfly returning home to God . . . which is a place where we are never alone, where we continue to grow and to sing and to dance, where we are with those we loved, and where we are surrounded with more love than we can ever imagine (*Wheel of Life,* p. 284; emphasis in original).*

Note: I have given Kübler-Ross more space and attention than some of the major philosophers, because I believe she had more life experience with the dying than most of, if not all, the others.

D. H. Lawrence (1885-1930)

English poet and novelist. Lawrence traveled widely outside England, in part because of a question of disloyalty surrounding him and his German-born wife. At the time of writing "Ship of Death" (extracts from which follow), he was aware of his own impending death from tuberculosis. He died in France.

The Ship of Death

> The apples falling like great drops of dew
> to bruise themselves an exit from themselves.

> And it is time to go, to bid farewell
> to one's self, and find an exit
> from the fallen self.

II

Have you built your ship of death, O have you?
O build your ship of death, for you will need it.

And in the bruised body, the frightened soul
finds itself shrinking, wincing from the cold
that blows upon it through the orifices.

III

And can a man his own quietus make
with a bare bodkin?

With daggers, bodkins, bullets, man can make
a bruise or break of exit for his life;
but is that a quietus, O tell me, is it quietus?
Surely not so! for how could murder, even self-murder
ever a quietus make?
. . . . . .

V

Build then the ship of death, for you must take
the longest journey, to oblivion.
And die the death, the long and painful death
that lies between the old self and the new.
Already our bodies are fallen, bruised, badly bruised.
already our souls are oozing through the exit
of the cruel bruise.

VI

We are dying, we are dying, piecemeal our bodies are dying
and our strength leaves us,
and our soul cowers naked in the dark rain over the flood,
cowering in the last branches of the tree of our life.

VII

We are dying, we are dying, so all we can do
is now to be willing to die, and to build the ship
of death to carry the soul on the longest journey.

Now launch the small ship, now as the body dies
and life departs, launch out, the fragile soul
in the fragile ship of courage, the ark of faith.

Edna St. Vincent Millay (1892-1950)

American poet. A Vassar graduate, Millay did most of her writing in Greenwich Village in the early 1920s. She and her husband lived most of their years together on a farm in New York State. "Dirge Without Music" is from *The Buck in the Snow and Other Poems* (1928).

Dirge Without Music

I am not resigned to the shutting away of loving hearts in the hard
   ground.
So it is, and so it will be, for so it has been, time out of mind:
Into the darkness they go, the wise and the lovely. Crowned
With lilies and with laurel they go; but I am not resigned.

Lovers and thinkers, into the earth with you.
Be one with the dull, the indiscriminate dust.
A fragment of what you felt, of what you knew,
A formula, a phrase remains,—but the best is lost.

The answers quick and keen, the honest look, the laughter, the
   love,—
They are gone. They are gone to feed the roses. Elegant and curled
Is the blossom. Fragrant is the blossom. I know. But I do not
   approve.
More precious was the light in your eyes than all the roses of the
   world.

Down, down, down into the darkness of the grave
Gently they go, the beautiful, the tender, the kind;
Quietly they go, the intelligent, the witty, the brave.
I know. But I do not approve. And I am not resigned.

Norman Vincent Peale (1898-1993)

American Protestant minister, radio preacher, and writer. He became pastor of Marble Collegiate church in New York in 1932 and held this position until the 1960s.

Peale wrote the highly successful *The Power of Positive Thinking* (1954). In another of his books, *Faith is the Answer* (1982), he has a section "Grief and Sorrow." Following up on St. Augustine's statement, Peale saw a vague restlessness in the human condition, a deep hunger for the eternal: "Our dead often evinced a deep, fundamental longing for something which this earth could not satisfy."

In *Faith,* Peale quotes a poem "World Strangeness" by William Watson, a poem he feels is so remarkable that a "stillness" came over those congregations to which he read it (from *Faith is The Answer,* pp. 149-150).

World Strangeness

Strange the world about me lies,
Never yet familiar grown
Still disturbs me with surprise,
Haunts me like a face half-known.

In his house with starry dome,
Floored with gem-like planes and seas,
Shall I never feel at home,
Never wholly be at ease?

On from room to room I stray;
Yet my host can ne'er espy,
And I know not to this day,
Whether guest or captive I.

So, between the starry dome
And the floor of planes and seas
I have never felt at home,
Never wholly been at ease.

William Shakespeare (1564-1616)

I will not waste space with biographical information on this man, one of the greatest figures in English literature. He certainly seems to have had some knowledge of Catholic theology, and the expression "shuffled off this mortal coil" indicates a knowledge of the Platonic or even Cartesian view of soul-body union and immortality.

In *Hamlet* (III, i) we have the famous reflections on exiting this life by one's own hand: "To be or not to be—that is the question." Avoiding the "slings and arrows" of this life is "a consummation / Devoutly to be wished . . . in that sleep of death what dreams may come / When we have shuffled off this mortal coil." Unfortunately, it is the "undiscovered country, from whose bourn / No traveler returns ("bourn" meaning boundary). Then we have Shakespeare's "grave-maker" who builds stronger than shipwrights and carpenters because the "houses he makes last till doomsday" (*Hamlet*, V, i).

Algernon C. Swinburne (1837-1909)

Major English poet. Swinburne attended Oxford but left to live a somewhat hedonistic lifestyle, which eventually led to a collapse in 1879. Strong hints of a death wish appear in his later work.

From "The Garden of Proserpine:"

> We are not sure of sorrow,
>   And joy was never sure;
> Today will die tomorrow;
>   Time stoops to no man's lure;
> And love, grown faint and fretful,
> With lips but half regretful
> Sighs, and with eyes forgetful
>   Weeps that no loves endure.
>
> From too much love of living,
>   From hope and fear set free,
> We thank with brief thanksgiving
>   Whatever gods may be
> That no life lives forever;
> That dead men rise up never;
> That even the weariest river
>   Winds somewhere safe to sea.

Alfred Lord Tennyson (1809-1892)

English poet. Tennyson was Baron of Aldworth. He attended Cambridge and in 1850 succeeded Wordsworth as poet laureate of England. His father was a clergyman in Lincolnshire, the place of his birth. In order to express his grief at the death of his friend Arthur Hallam, he wrote his famous elegy.

From "In Memoriam" (1850) (emphasis added):

> Strong Son of God, immortal Love
>   Whom we, that have not seen thy face,
>   By faith, and faith alone, embrace,
> Believing where we cannot prove;
>
> Thine are these orbs of light and shade;
>   Thou madest Life in man and brute;
>   Thou madest Death; and, thy foot
> Is on the skull which thou has made.
>
> Thou wilt not leave us in the dust:
>   Thou madest man, he knows not why,
>   He thinks he was not made to die;
> And thou hast made him: thou art just.
>
> We have but faith: we cannot know,
>   For knowledge is of things we see;
>   And yet we trust it comes from thee,
> A beam in darkness: let it grow.

Forgive my grief for one removed,
  Thy creature, whom I found so fair.
  I trust he lives in thee, and there
I find him worthier to be loved.

Note: This is a lengthy poem and the reader might choose other quatrains.

Sherwin Nuland (1995) quotes Tennyson in *How We Die* (p. 86):

Old men die, or the world would grow moldy, would only breed the past again.

Norman Vincent Peale (1982) also quotes him (from "Maud, A Mono-drama, Part III") in his book *Faith is the Answer:*

Ah, Christ! If it were possible for one short hour to see the souls we loved, that they might tell us what and where they lie.

Leo Tolstoy (1828-1910)

Russian novelist. Among Tolstoy's most famous books are *War and Peace, Anna Karenina,* and *The Death of Ivan Ilyich.* Like many others included in this book, he was raised in a religious tradition but fell away from it as he entered adulthood. His writings brought him fame, property, and a fair amount of wealth with which he was able to raise his family in comfort.

However, for whatever reason, Tolstoy began to question the purpose of his existence and even that of his children. What do we live for? To eat? To propagate? It all seemed meaningless and therefore raised the question: why go on with such a farce? What philosophers term "The Great Questions" began to absorb his thinking, and he sought answers from so-called "men of wisdom."

Considerations of suicide and his morbid attitude toward death were eventually set aside as Tolstoy realized that adherents of the Christian faith who were deeply religious seemed satisfied with their lives, could endure their sufferings, and were content in spite of their poverty and ignorance. The teachings of Christ, of love for each other, charity toward the poor—even adopting a peasant way of life (which he did)—finally gave meaning to his life. Although he considered faith a denial of reason, in the end he seems to have resolved his dilemma in favor of faith.

Note: I wonder whether he was aware that thinkers such as Augustine and Aquinas had also wrestled with this problem of reconciling faith and reason: "Fides quaerens intellecta" (faith seeking to be understood).

CHAPTER 4
Grief and Bereavement

One aspect of human makeup is the emotions. Some refer to the emotions (or passions) as the irrational side of our nature and divide them into the concupiscible and the irascible. The concupiscible would be love, desire, and joy and their opposites hatred, aversion, and sorrow. The irascible deal with frustration of our desires—anger, fear, anxiety, and so forth.

The grieving and bereaved are in a state of sorrow, but they can also be angry or anxious, depending on their situation. What they wanted to avoid has now come upon them. They are bereft of a loved one.

It could be argued that in a way, grieving begins with the diagnosis of a terminal illness. In her famous book *On Death and Dying* (1969), Dr. Elisabeth Kübler-Ross gave us the five reactions people often experience after receiving this news and as the illness intensifies: denial, anger, bargaining (with God), depression, and, perhaps, final acceptance. Not all are necessarily present, and the order can vary. Different authors have come up with different perspectives on these responses (see e.g., Charles Carr's book in Suggested Readings later in this chapter).

Whether the death is sudden or comes after a long struggle, survivors are usually in a state of shock and disorganization. Some call this "reactive grief." A person who was significant in our life has left us for the remainder of it. We might also experience existential grief—the realization that ultimately our own life is only temporary and one day we too will experience dying and will be waked and buried.

However, psychologists think that relatives are usually more concerned about *surviving* the loved one's death. Robert Kavanaugh (1972) sees other stages of grief occurring besides shock and disorganization. One stage might be guilt, for a variety of reasons—perhaps we didn't do enough or we feel a sense of relief that the end has finally come. Another stage could be loneliness, a strong sense of loss, but hopefully followed by reestablishment.

Authors and experts in this field give the following advice. Those who are grieving should understand that their condition is nothing to be ashamed of. They have suffered and will continue to suffer wrenching loss, vague confusion, perhaps unrelenting sadness at missing a loved one's physical presence, as well as loneliness, a devastating numbness, and even despair. They might feel that nothing matters anymore or that nothing will ever be the same (on this they could very well be right).

Holiday times, of course, will be very difficult to get through, as will anniversaries and birthdays. Family should try to lessen the loneliness and depression at these times and hope that with the passing of time, these occasions will be endured more easily. Some special or different activity should be scheduled for these difficult days.

There is no set period of time for grieving. Expressions of anger and sadness are to be expected, but if the person goes into deep despair, cannot function or stays in bed for a long period, then family and friends must put out maximum effort to arrange for professional help.

Psychologists urge a return to everyday tasks and work as soon as possible. Changes in lifestyle, the use of support groups, joining an organization, doing charitable work, and taking on new relationships can all be helpful.

In other words, what is needed is a gradual "letting go" while being assured by clergy, relatives, and friends that "letting go" does *not* mean forgetting. Each person must heal at his or her own pace. Healing is a process. In response to demanding friends the grieving person could reply, "Be patient. God (or nature) hasn't finished healing me yet."

As I mentioned in the Introduction, grieving is somewhat complex because it takes place in what one might call "diverse combinations." There is the grieving of the widow and of the widower; of children who have lost a young parent or an elderly parent; of parents who have lost a child by disease, by accident, or by war. I have also included in this chapter a case of a grieving brother and his letter home to his mother from a Civil War battlefield. (The soldier himself was to die after writing this poignant letter home.) The brief observations given here are gathered from the writings of authors and experts in the field. However, we should keep in mind that these writers do not always agree.

Let us now consider the various situations.

DEATH OF A HUSBAND

I have already mentioned the case of a newly ordained priest posing what he later considered a stupid question to a young widow, who proceeded to berate him in front of everyone at the wake. Kübler-Ross tells us of young clergy seeking advice on dealing with grieving survivors.

Assess the situation. How familiar are you with the family? What should you definitely avoid saying? Was it a good marriage? Does the widow have support around her? Are there children—especially grown children? Are the widow's parents still alive and able to lend support? Does she have siblings or friends who can be with her at this time?

In what financial condition has she been left? Does she have a profession or some way to make a living? Can she return to a job and immerse herself in her work with the companionship of fellow workers?

After a certain period of time, the somewhat sensitive question of the possibility of remarriage might be raised.

From the moment of the death to the moment of the dispersal of family and friends following the funeral (and perhaps a luncheon at a restaurant or someone's home), the widow is immersed in details and the rituals of convention. However, when the funeral events are finally over she must face her future, which may entail temporary or even permanent loneliness (which is different from "aloneness") and perhaps financial hardship.

Christian preachers usually concentrate on "reunion" in the next life. This belief applies to all cases of bereavement, so I will postpone this topic until later.

DEATH OF A WIFE

Much of what I have just said could also be said of the widower. The grief of a husband for a dead wife can be very profound and the bereavement long-lasting. Many widowers never remarry. The man has lost his best friend and companion; the "bride of his youth" in many cases; the woman who threw in her lot with him as they struggled in the early days of the marriage; the woman who bore their children and had faith that he would support and protect her and their children to the best of his ability. (Disbelief at the death of a *young* wife could almost put the husband in a state of shock.)

On a more mundane level, the widower might very well be bereft of someone who took care of the home and finances, someone who worked and even earned a higher salary. This loss of income could be devastating to the financial situation and lifestyle of the husband and perhaps young children. Often, most of the family life insurance is on the husband. If he must go off to a full day's work, day care for young children could be quite expensive. (This same situation, of course, could also occur for a widow.)

On the other hand, a man usually has better opportunities for remarriage. He can go out alone to restaurants, bars, dances, and so forth more easily than can a woman, given our customs and our society's danger quotient. Quite often he is the main wage earner, and even if he does not make a "high" salary he might find a woman who does.

Nevertheless, I think the Tom Hanks character in the movie *Sleepless in Seattle* showed us the more common reality regarding the loss of a man's beloved wife and the mother of his child. He eventually moved away from everything familiar; and I don't think even a Meg Ryan could cause a man to forget the years and events of a wonderful marriage.

DEATH OF A CHILD

Before addressing the grieving of parents for their child, I would like to consider what could be a concomitant issue. Should very young children be told they have a terminal condition? By very young I mean children who have not as yet had enough life experience to distinguish diseases that are usually fatal from those that are not. "Experts" in this area are not in total agreement. I personally believe that since a young child has no "affairs" to be put in order, be they spiritual or material, there is no necessity to inform him or her and thus open up the difficulties of explanation—although I once read about a dying child who wrote a brief "will" in which he left his toys and pets to various people.

Many authors think that young children will begin to suspect that something is terribly wrong with them because of the favorable treatment they are receiving from family and doctors. Therefore, they believe we should wait for the questions to come and tailor the answers to the intellectual level and degree of sophistication of the child.

If the child has had a religious upbringing, then, of course, a discussion of life, death, resurrection, God, and heaven can be quite helpful for the child—especially the notion of reunion with loved ones in heaven.

Clergy, nurses, and doctors must be careful to respect whatever path the family wishes to take. If directly asked by the child, "Am I going to die from this disease?" I think one answer could be "I have no idea" or "I cannot say." Not everyone dies because they have ____." This is a somewhat evasive answer but not necessarily a lie. People with AIDS are living longer. Cancer goes into remission. "Miracles" of nature *do* happen, and clergy should certainly believe that miracles in the supernatural sense (suspension of the effect of a law of nature in a particular case by the power of God) are possible. Besides, it is only when the child has actually died that a doctor or nurse can be absolutely certain that a specific condition will lead to a termination of life.

What consolations can be given to the parents of a dying child or following the death of their child? I think parents who have a strong religious faith in God and in His will for the salvation of all persons would realize that an innocent child has attained or will attain this ultimate goal of human existence. The child already is or will be in God's presence and protection forever and parents of strong faith may accept this as an act of God's tolerative will.

And while realistically the parent's realize that their child will not endure the various sufferings of adult life they are also aware of the many joys they will miss. (Elisabeth Kübler-Ross mentions some of these in her book *On Children and Death.*) Naturally, parents would have preferred to risk these sufferings if God or fate had dealt them a different hand. But it was not to be. Their child is at peace in the presence of God, and as Dan Ackroyd said after the death of John Belushi, none of us is far behind.

A few years ago the baby of radio producer Joel Hollander was found dead in her crib—a case of SIDS, sudden infant death syndrome. A colleague and radio personality, Don Imus, went immediately to the Hollander home to offer support and was profoundly affected by the death. Since then Imus has worked diligently and successfully to secure funds for research on this phenomenon. He recently mentioned that the other Hollander children are *still* emotionally affected by the death of their infant sibling.

Dr. Elisabeth Kübler-Ross, in her 1983 book entitled *On Children and Death,* points out that time allows us to recover from the shock and numbness following the death of a young person. We need time to react to what she calls the "little deaths" which take place before the final separation. By this term she means the physical consequences of chemotherapy, the inability to play sports, go to a prom or bring home friends. Eventually, there is the realization we will never see them graduate or wear a wedding gown, "and their families mourn these things that will never be."

One final note on young siblings—they can react to the dying or death of a brother or sister in different ways. Some might become jealous of the attention given to the sick child. Yet, they also live in a house of "chronic sorrow" and might even believe that *they* caused the illness because of bad behavior. We must assure all children (the sick child and the siblings) that *nothing* they have done has brought about this situation. These feelings merit the attention of parents and clergy. (*The Asbury Park Press* had an article several years ago about a 13-year-old cancer patient at Sloan-Kettering who shortly before he died said, "I'm sorry God.")

DEATH OF A PARENT

The Elderly Parent

Again, clergy and others must use caution here. The temptation is to think, or even express the thought, that if the deceased is perhaps 70 or over he or she has "had a good run." Objectively speaking this would be hard to deny, especially when we think of all the young who have died in war, in accidents, and from disease. However, again objectively speaking, the death of an elderly parent can be a wrenching loss if the relationship has been loving and close. Also, the death may have been preceded by a long and painful dying process which has aggravated the situation.

Deep down, of course, all reasonable people anticipate the death of a parent after a certain age, but anyone can be taken by surprise when the person is discovered to have a fatal disease. And seemingly healthy people can die suddenly.

Another consideration, as always, is the joy of living, or lack thereof, which the deceased had experienced. What was the quality of their life—physical, mental, and emotional? Were they financially comfortable? If not, what assistance had to be given to them? Can clergy find out the nature of the relationship between parent and children over the years? Were they close? Friendly? Might there by some guilt feelings on the part of the child? Before making statements or posing questions at a wake or making potentially embarrassing remarks in a homily, it would be wise to at least *try* to ascertain the "story" on the family situation.

Nevertheless, speakers at a wake or funeral can certainly mention the gift of long life that the deceased had enjoyed (but should the word "enjoyed" be used?) but also make clear that this fact cannot fully console the children and can even make the final separation more difficult. *Hopefully,* one can mention the parent's joy and satisfaction in the gift of children and the pride in the children's lives. I say "hopefully" because we all know that sometimes there has been a so-called "falling out."

If you feel you are on treacherous ground, it might be wiser to stay with generalities such as immortality, reunion in heaven where all hurts will be healed, and so forth. In all these matters the faith of the family and their emotional condition become very important.

The Young Parent

Here again, there is a wide variety of situations to be assessed by clergy and speakers. Which parent are we talking about? Girls will miss their mothers for a variety of reasons—many of them practical; yet, they can be very emotionally attracted to their fathers. All children will worry about who will take care of them, and of the whole family, if the person they see as the "breadwinner" has died. They also wonder whether they will be able to remain in their home. These are usually the practical fears of children over the age of eight.

Professionals in this field of psychology think the explanation of death should be tailored to the age of the child. Longer books and textbooks go into great detail, but for the purposes of this manual, I think the following will suffice.

Children under Ten

Various questions arise. Is my father or mother asleep? If so, when will he wake up? Why isn't she coming back? (This is asked when a parent has often been away on business trips.) If he "went to heaven" why is he in this "box"? What's going to happen to me? Adults should try to make the children feel secure. Even in a religious home, these young children are not yet ready for the idea of body-soul union or separation, and they often try to "visualize" their parent in heaven.

Age Ten through the Teens

The concept of the soul and the afterlife should be more understandable for these children. There will be the realization that death is final. Fear and anxiety will enter their life, tied in somewhat with existential grief. As Dr. John Morgan pointed out in his article, "A Philosopher Looks at Children and Death,": "Once children know about death, their world is irreparably altered. This is one of the most difficult lessons one must learn. Yet it is only in the realization of the limits of our resources that we can get the most from their use. It is only in the realization of the limits of life that we appreciate the fullness of life" (pp. 165-166). Now it is important to stress the soul's survival and the belief that the parent has achieved the end or destiny that is the ultimate life-purpose for all of us. (I don't know whether the term "our fate" should be used.) Death—its necessity and timing—as a mystery for all living things can be discussed.

On the practical side, pointing out a kind of "responsibility: to assist the surviving parent, if there is one, might help the children through the grieving process, keep them occupied with various tasks and discussions—"talking things out." Authors believe the children will eventually start asking questions.

Finally, the continued presence of extended family and friends is important—not just through the funeral period, but for an indeterminate time to come.

DEATH OF A SIBLING

The following is an excerpt from an unpublished history of the Hallock family, one branch of which lived in Milton, New York, in the lower Hudson Valley. "Mother Hallock's" married name was Ketcham; her sons were Edward and John. Although Quakers, they fought in the Civil War because of the "evil of slavery." Edward was killed by a sniper's bullet, and John was captured and died of disease contracted from the unsanitary conditions in a Confederate prison (Libby Prison, Richmond, Virginia). In these letters, John attempts to console his mother over the death of his brother Edward, while at the same time suffering profound grief himself.[1]

Frederick City, July 8, 1863

Dear Mother:

I telegraphed to thee as soon as I could, and wrote about Edward. I cannot realize that he is dead. Don't let it kill thee, Mother! Thee and I are all that is left of us. Edward was the first man killed in the regiment. . . . a sharpshooter's bullet probably struck him in the temple. . . . He put up his hand, and said, "Oh!" and fell on his elbow, quite dead. . . . I heard of it the next morning, and went to the regiment, and got a man to go with me, who helped to carry him off; showed me where he lay. . . .

I went out at night to look for Edward, but could not find him. The next morning our line advanced, and I went out to the tree: and there, on his back, his hands peacefully on his breast, lay all that was left of the brother I have lived so closely with, all my life. . . . And mother, thee and I walk this world of sorrow. . . . Mother, yet a little time thee and I have to walk this earth, when we compare it to the great eternity beyond, where Father and Edward are gone before us.

---

[1] This material was sent to me by my sister-in-law, Judy Comeau Talarczyk, who lived in Milton at the time of her death.

Oh, he was cut down in the very morning of his manhood! . . . laid a sacrifice on the altar of Liberty! He died to give every other man the right to his own manhood—a precious sacrifice. . . . He died as he would have died, with his face towards the enemies of freedom, on the battle-field. . . . Oh, God! Thy price for freedom is a Dear One!

John

Near Sharpsburg, July 12th, 1863

Dear Mother,

. . . Keep heart and courage, mother: he has only gone beyond us. It is a comfort to think that his suffering was so short. . . . One instant of terrible pain, and the life which he loved, as all strong men do, faded from his sense, and was changed for the great Hereafter, when all human imperfection is changed for perfection. Brother! our paths through life have run side by side, diverging but to join again. Now you have the better part, above the petty strifes of this life.

John

Harper's Ferry, July 19th, 1863

Dear Mother:

. . . My comfort is that Edward died as becomes a man, his face towards the enemies of freedom. . . . I can do or say nothing to comfort my poor stricken mother. In thy boundless love for thy children, thy bereavement is more than mine, lonely and sad as I am, "wretch even now, life's journey just begun."

After John's death, the two brothers were brought back to Milton and buried in the Friends cemetery, side by side. A somewhat famous Unitarian minister, the Rev. O. B. Frothingham, came to Milton to deliver the funeral oration. The family historian, a Mr. Duganne, tells us that he was probably "congenial" to the Hicksite Quakers who formed the Milton Meeting chapter. Here are some excerpts from the address:

It is a strange sight, the coffin of a soldier, wrapped in a battle-flag lying in a Friends' meeting-house. He was educated a Friend, and was in spirit, to the end, one of that peaceful brotherhood, who abhor violence and blood-shedding and war. Comfort yourselves, oh, Friends, with the thought that he preserved that pious abhorrence as sacredly as you do. He was a lover of peace; he went out in the holy cause of peace, as a peacemaker. Not to make war, or to continue war, but to put an end to war; to die himself, if need were, by the hand of war, that war might cease. To make war in his country forever impossible, by eradicating human slavery, its permanent cause, he took up arms. There seemed no other way of doing it. He would thankfully have used other means, had other means been permitted. Accepting these, he prayed always for the quiet rest he hoped these would bring. You need not be afraid of shocking your principles by receiving him here from battle. . . .

O my friends, the time is coming, the time is surely coming, when all they who went down into this great struggle will be held in honor by all lovers of order and peace; . . . when they who, like this young man, have died in it, with a noble sense of its significance, will be reckoned among the martyrs of God's truth.

SUGGESTED READINGS

Charles Carr, Ph.D. "A Task-Based Approach to Coping with Dying." In *The Path Ahead—Readings in Death and Dying,* Lynne DeSpelder and Albert Strickland (eds.). Mayfield, Mountain View, CA, 1955. Here we are told that people should take charge of their own death—recognizing that it has physical, psychological, social, and spiritual dimensions.

Melba Colgrove, Ph.D., Harold Bloomfield, M.D., and Peter McWilliams. *How to Survive the Loss of a Love.* Prelude Press, Los Angeles, CA, 1991.

Victoria Frigo, Diane Fischer, and Mary Lou Cook. *You Can Help Someone Who's Grieving.* Penguin Books, New York, NY, 1996.

Joan Rivers. *Bouncing Back.* Famous as a comedienne, Rivers is a well-educated woman. She was devastated by the suicide of her husband. She gives a very moving account of the emotional and economic fallout from his death—for her, her daughter, and her career. She also gives those who are grieving some practical advice on survival and the role that humor can play.

SUPPLEMENTARY TEXTS

Robert Buckman:
I Don't Know What to Say (1988)

Dr. Buckman is a cancer specialist at Sunnybrook Hospital, University of Toronto, and has been active in radio and television in Great Britain and Canada.

Why do we get angry when we're ill? The single most important reason is loss of control. The problem is that illness *doesn't* happen our way. It happens its own way. There are several kinds of anger that people experience and they can be divided into three major types:

1. *Anger at the rest of the world,* including friends and relatives and everybody who isn't ill, all of whom are going to carry on living. (You could call this the "why me?" anger.)
2. *Anger directed at any recognizable form of fate,* or destiny, or controlling influence that has allowed this to happen. (In people who have religious beliefs, this anger may be directed at God, or may cause a loss of religious faith.)
3. *Anger at anyone who is trying to help,* particularly doctors and nurses. (This is the "blaming the bearer for the bad news" reaction.) . . .
4. FEAR

Fear of serious illness and death are so common (in our society at least) that we would normally regard someone who was not frightened as crazy.

Not only is fear very common, but most of us are brought up to be *afraid of being afraid,* or at least, to be ashamed of being afraid. In a way, most of us have an idea at the back of our minds that we're not *supposed* to be afraid of things.

First, to be afraid, you have to have imagination. . . . Second, fear of dying is not one fear but many fears. . . . There are fears to do with physical illness and incapacity, fears of being handicapped, of being a burden to friends and family, and of being unable to contribute to family life.

There are fears about physical pain, "How much suffering will there be, and how will I stand up to it? . . . Then there are fears that are sometimes called "existential" fears, about the ending of life itself—the end of existence. And spiritual fears: "What happens afterwards? Will there simply be oblivion? Will there be an afterlife and could there be punishment?" . . .

HOPE, DESPAIR, AND DEPRESSION

Facing up to the possibility (or probability) of the end of life is a monumental task for the patient. It seems to be the worst thing that could possibly happen, and that once the hope of a longer, healthy life has gone, there is nothing except despair.

Despair, like anger, fear, and denial, is a very common phase in facing the threat of dying. There is no magic formula that will instantly banish it. The word "despair" really means the "loss of hope."

Usually despair comes and goes in cycles. Like the shock reaction, despair is an emotion that tends to overwhelm the patient for a time, then partially fade, and then return, and so on. No one knows precisely why that is. I have postulated that it is because the human mind is an adaptive system and does not function very well under extremes of emotion. Hence (in my view) our minds are programmed to find a balance, and to return to a normal state as soon as possible after a large emotional shock.

You also need to be aware . . . that despair can never be cured by false hope . . . (pp. 44-49).

THE STAGES OF GRIEVING

Grieving is a continuous process. It is continuous just as the transition that the patient makes from being healthy to facing the end of life is continuous. For the sake of convenience, I shall divide grieving into three stages: an initial stage, a middle stage, and a resolution stage.

THE INITIAL STAGE OF GRIEF

The initial phase of grief is often like shock. Bereaved relatives use words like, "numb," "in shock," and "dazed," to describe it.

The shock is often followed by deep sadness. During the deep sadness, you will probably find that you cry a great deal or feel like crying every time that the dead person's name is mentioned, or some memory of her crops up.

THE MIDDLE STAGE OF GRIEF

The middle stage of grief is the phase during which you begin to realize that life will go on after your bereavement, even though you may not yet see how. It may begin a few weeks after death, but if you have been through a lot of anticipatory grief, it may begin sooner. During this phase, the shock and numbing begin to fade away, and life begins to regain some semblance of normality.

You may look all right, but you may be feeling very far from all right. Grieving relatives and spouses have described this phase to me as "hollow," "feeling like a sham," "feeling like a ghost," "not being there."

THE RESOLUTION PHASE

Not every authority on grieving thinks the same way about the resolution of grief. However, it is reasonable to suggest that grief has been resolved when the survivor is able to remember the person who has died with fondness and pleasure, is able to recall the good moments and to think about them without acute pain and distress, although (perhaps) with some regret. Resolution has something to do with being (in a way) whole again, and living an independent life—although it is not the *same* life as before the bereavement (pp. 108-114).*

---

*Reprinted with the permission of author from *I Don't Know What to Say* by Dr. Robert Buckman. [Copyright © Robert Buckman, 1988, 1996.]

In the final sections of his book, Dr. Buckman gives practical advice for handling the various situations I have mentioned "After the Bereavement," as he puts it—after the death of a spouse, a parent, a child, and a sibling. For example, following the death of a spouse:

AFTER THE BEREAVEMENT

Starting life again after the loss of your spouse is a daunting prospect. . . . From what I have already said about the grieving process . . . I think I would emphasize the following steps:

1. *Accept the way you feel.*
2. *Assess your needs.*
3. *List your resources.*
4. *Don't make big decisions rapidly.*
5. *Get help if you need it* (p. 154; emphasis in original)

Earl Grollman (Ed.):
Bereaved Children and Teens (1995)

This extract is from the article by Rabbi Earl Grollman, D.D.

Explaining Death to Young Children

Q: Do children really grieve?
A: Yes. Grief is an expression of love. Mourning is an appropriate emotion for people of all ages. Children are no strangers to unhappy feelings—they know what it means to feel mad, sad, guilty, lonely, and afraid.

Children's responses to grief fluctuate according to their concepts of death, their developmental level, their relationship with the person who died, the circumstances surrounding the death, and the ability of caregivers to communicate with and emotionally support them. Some children may refuse to speak about the individual who died; others will speak of nothing else. Some will talk of the death at unexpected times—even months and years later. Some will cry uncontrollably; others will remain outwardly impassive and emotionless; others may even laugh. Some will praise the loved one as the most wonderful person in the whole world; others will hate the individual for abandoning them. Some will blame themselves for the death; others will project their grief on God, the physician, the religious leader, the funeral director, or members of the family. Children's despair may be interrupted by a carefree mood, vacillating between sadness and playful joy. Reactions are varied and contradictory—and usually predictable.

Children must not be deprived of the right to grieve. They should no more be excluded from sharing grief and sorrow than they should be prevented from demonstrating joy and happiness. Each person, adult and child, should be given the opportunity to lament the end of life in his or her own way. Too often, well-meaning people say, "Be brave! Don't cry! Don't take it so hard." Children should never be discouraged from crying in order to express their grief. Weeping helps express the despair that follows the slow realization that the death is not a bad dream. Don't be afraid to cry in front of children. One of the most loving experiences that adults and children can share is weeping together to express the pain of separation (p. 9).*

Kenneth J. Doka: Friends, Teachers, Movie Stars: The Disenfranchised Grief of Children.

Kenneth J. Doka, Ph.D., is professor of gerontology at the College of New Rochelle.

THE DISENFRANCHISED GRIEF OF CHILDREN

Like adults, children too, can be disenfranchised grievers, often for the very same reasons. Like the rest of us, children have a circle of people with whom they are exceedingly close.

The death of a friend can be devastating. Not only is it a frightening reminder of vulnerability and mortality, but it is also the loss of a key relationship, a part of the child's identity. Children will grieve these losses intensely. But the adults around them may not recognize the great significance of the loss.

Even negative attachments can be grieved, when the relationship is a strong one. Louie was an aggressive, sometimes bullying sixth grader. When he died in a car accident, his teacher was surprised that one of the children most affected was Keith, a child Louie often tormented. Keith felt very guilty about the death since he often had publicly wished Louie would die or disappear.

The deaths or illnesses of rock stars, presidents, or other heroes may cause a deep sense of grief. Many adolescent youths, for example, grieved with Magic Johnson when he announced he was infected with HIV.

Another kind of unrecognized loss is an abortion. Not everyone who has an abortion experiences a grief reaction, but some do.

One of the most common, most significant, and often unrecognized losses in adolescence is the loss of a romantic relationship, breakups of boyfriends and girlfriends. In his surveys of college freshman, Louis LaGrand . . . found that this was the loss cited as most significant by the largest number of respondents. Many adults, however, were unresponsive to the feelings of grief that such breakups generated.

Even graduations can be ambivalent experiences encompassing both pride and loss.

Divorce can represent a major loss for many children. It is often complicated by the fact that children may have many ambivalent feelings about divorce, for example, regretting the separation but being happy that any open conflict has ended.

It is true that young children or developmentally or mentally impaired adolescents may express grief differently from older children. . . . Their grief then may be expressed in short intensive outbursts followed by periods during which they seem unaffected by loss. But, while young children or developmentally or mentally impaired youths may grieve differently, they still grieve.

Finally, there are disenfranchising deaths. Children are not immune to shame, and certain types of deaths carry a stigma that children may hesitate to bear (pp. 40-43).*

John D. Morgan: A Philosopher Looks at Children and Death.

John D. Morgan, Ph.D., is professor of philosophy at King's College of the University of Western Ontario and senior editor of many volumes of the *Death, Value and Meaning* series for the Baywood Publishing Company.

Perhaps the greatest single element in the formation of our attitudes toward death is the perception of the *person as unique*. In the Western world today, we are seemingly more conscious of our individuality than in other parts of the world and other historical eras. We believe that there is a self hidden within each of us that no list of characteristics captures, what Becker refers to as "the ache of cosmic specialness." The dominant philosophy of education is existentialism, with its stress on feeling good about oneself.

The effect of an increased life span and a lessened exposure to death is a lowered consciousness of and respect for the power of death. We know that death exists. Our lifetime has seen more deaths than the entire previous history of the human race. We have lived in the shadow of the Holocaust and of nuclear destruction. We accept the abstraction of even our own death. Indeed, the evidence is that college students think about death more often than did their grandparents. But we do not have an *affective consciousness* of death. We do not seem to accept the *real probability* of death, much less its *appropriateness*. . . .

*From *Bereaved Children and Teens,* by Earl a. Grollman, Copyright © 1995 by Earl A. Grollman. Reprinted by permission of Beacon Press, Boston.

Children and Death
The Death of Children

As I have shown above, our basic philosophical orientation is that we live in a predictable world. We believe that the universe is governed by God for our benefit. However, there are two flaws in this model. First of all, only a limited part of the human experience can be thought of as orderly. In particular, death is not evenly distributed. The aged die, and unfortunately they often die alone because we have defined our lives without them. The poor, the racially discriminated against, and the poorly educated die earlier than do other members of the North American culture. Violence is a daily phenomenon in every city, large and small, of North America, yet we still pretend that life goes on in predictable, orderly ways.

Death Education of Children

It is clear that the death attitude system most prevalent in North America today does not provide persons with the tools they need at the time of a death. We need to accept the reality that, each time we say "goodbye" to someone, it could very well be the last time—and teach our children the same. All relations are time limited. When we educate children about death, we are only teaching them reality. Death is not just a possibility; it is a certainty for all of us.

The Trappist monks have a saying that one does not have one's feet on the ground until after one has put someone into it. It is wrong to hide this truth from our children. They will learn that truth. It should not be in spite of the adults who care for them (pp. 164-166; emphasis in original).*

I recommend a reading of this entire book, but especially the views from three major religions: the Protestant perspective by Richard Gilbert, the Catholic by Mary Ann McLaughlin, and the Jewish by Rabbi Earl Grollman.

Lynn Caine: *Being a Widow* (1988)

Lynn Caine is also the author of the best-seller *Widow* (1974). Of *Being a Widow,* Caine said "I wish I had been able to turn to [this book] when Martin died!" Caine herself died of cancer in December 1987.

Caine recorded that in her first book, Widow, she examined what she referred to as the stages of widowhood. These paralleled Kübler-Ross' stages of emotions of people facing terminal illness and widows will

---

*From *Bereaved Children and Teens,* by Earl A. Grollman, Copyright © 1995 by Earl A. Grollman. Reprinted by permission of Beacon Press, Boston.

react to these feelings, including "panic," in their own way and bereavement counselors must realize this,

> The stages of grief can overlap . . . or can show up in an order different from that presented here. There is no such thing as normal grief . . .

She had listed "numbness" first and proceeded through seven more stages to "acceptance." Caine recognized that widowhood can have degrees of difficulty depending upon the situation in which she is left (as I pointed out in the main body of this book). However, she still felt that "there is no better or worse way to lose a husband."

> . . . a phone call and my life was forever changed.

This book contains many more sections that give practical advice on continued grieving, creating a new social life, problems associated with renewal of a sexual life, returning to the workforce, and hopes for the future.

Linda Alderman:
Why Did Daddy Die? (1989)

Widowed by the death of Don Alderman in 1982, Linda Alderman has formed and facilitated groups for widowed parents in New Jersey and Michigan as well as teaching psychology at the College of New Jersey. She married Dan Gray in 1987.

> The fourth phase of grief, depression, seems to last forever, and, indeed, to some extent it does. Even in acceptance, long after one has put together a new life, depression can be triggered by a season, a holiday, or any other time when the longing for a loved one seems overwhelming. More than overlapping the previous phases, it is the undercurrent from which they are trying to protect us. Slivers of sadness pierce those defense mechanisms of shock and denial, anger, and bargaining from the beginning of our bereavement. Over time, those defenses loosen, and the dominant feelings become sadness and longing (p. 126).
>
> As with adults, children's longing never completely fades. Parents are forever missed each time these young people take a new step in their growth and understanding. Each important event, each passage in their lifetimes, is another that parent and child might have shared together. We will always be sad at times, because, as Lara [Alderman's daughter] put it, "We used to have a big family. Now we have a small one" (p. 144).
>
> My children's struggle to accept their father's death began almost immediately after he died and continued in a long sometimes erratic

progression. Acceptance was, after all, the period of grief to which all other phases were leading.

Even in the midst of other phases, there were times when Marc [Alderman's son] and Lara seemed to possess an amazingly mature serenity as they pondered their father's death. . . . One of Lara's earliest moments of acceptance was only a month after Don died. She'd just awakened from a nap and lay in her cozy bed, a particularly secure place for Lara, clutching her tattered pink blanket. As she and I snuggled warmly, she eulogized Don with still sleepy words: "We only have one daddy in the whole wide world."

"Yes," I agreed.

"Daddy wanted to stay here forever and ever," she told me.

"Yes, but he couldn't," I reminded her.

"Because he died," she said (p. 146).

Bereaved children who ask why their parent died need to be told the physical cause of death, no matter how unpleasant it may be for the surviving parent to explain. By explaining the cause of death as a car accident or heart failure rather than invoking the intervention of God, children may be better able to grasp the idea that God is standing by to help us with love, in good times and in bad.

I'd been thinking about religious education for my children for a few months, and after taking that first step, the next step— finding a home church for our family—came easily. One Sunday I visited the local church of the denomination in which I had been raised. I was so warmly welcomed that by the next Sunday the children were enrolled in Sunday school and the Sunday after that I was wearing a choir robe. I was amazed not only at how comfortable I felt but also at how suddenly my anger with God had dissipated (pp. 202-203).

As Marc, Lara and I formed our relationship with the church, our spiritual concept of death finally evolved into one we could hold in common. We were comforted by sharing a belief that Don was with God in heaven. Although the way Marc and Lara came to understand that concept might have been somewhat unorthodox, they seemed to grasp intuitively the beliefs that adults write books arguing over. Because they believed God is everywhere, they found no incongruity in believing that Don's spirit could be both in heaven and with us. He commuted (p. 205).*

Fr. Dominic Fuccile:
"A Pastor Expresses His Grief" (1999)

Fr. Dominic Fuccile wrote this piece on the death of the father of his parochial vicar, Fr. Frank Rocchi.

This past week has been a very full one for me. With it came a full range of emotions. I shared in the loss of my friend's father. It has been close enough to my own loss to feel again with Father Frank what that loss is like. I mourned with him and his family, while at the same time I shared in their relief that Ferruccio was finally at peace, no more suffering. I felt very close to Father Frank. I could understand fully his own need to mourn, to just be a son who has lost a father and fully feel that loss. And yet he is called upon to be the one who supports everyone else. Where to find the right words to say and then have the courage to say them. It has to be the hardest thing to do, to speak at a parent's funeral Mass. Father Frank paid a wonderful tribute to his father. Those of us who did not know him very well came to understand the loss his family felt at the death of this simple man who loved his family and claimed many as his friends. Father Frank and his family are in my thoughts and prayers these difficult days.

Suicide and Euthanasia

SUICIDE

The survivors of someone who has committed suicide will be left with many questions, most of which may go forever unanswered. *Why* did she take her life? Could anyone have prevented it? Did we miss the "signs"? Was he in his "right mind"? Religious people might be concerned with the question of moral responsibility, because the act obviously called for some premeditation.

Counselors can point out several things that might console survivors. First, "amateurs" usually are not capable of recognizing the "signs" of a potential suicide. Even psychiatrists "lose" their patients. Second, "premeditation" does not necessarily mean a totally free-will act. The deeper question is *why* did the person set up the equipment and conditions necessary for the act. Finally, some philosophers and psychologists take the position of "soft determinism" that is, while we might have some degree of free will, this doesn't mean we are totally free from the influence of family, religion, society, and even our genetic inheritance. Some speak of "unconscious motivations," whereas premeditation would be on the conscious level of the mind.

Nevertheless, authors on the subject say we should never think that those who talk about suicide have no real intention of committing suicide. If possible, relatives, friends, and counselors should talk it out with them, try to find the root cause of their depression or despair, and see whether the situation can be rectified. It is, of course, the hidden "personal demons" that are the most difficult to discover and deal with.

Clergy and others should advise the survivors not to judge the potential or actual suicide harshly, and as clergy, you should make it clear that neither you nor the church you represent are going to come to conclusions about moral guilt—all of this, however *only* if the question is raised.

Objectively, of course, suicide is a morally serious act. It is final. There is no coming back from it. God gave us a wondrous gift and expects a responsible stewardship over it. It is His right to determine the time, place, and manner of our death. Again, objectively speaking, we might say that the act of suicide is a usurpation of that right.

Naturally, if suicide is objectively evil, those who assist someone to exit this life have committed what is called "cooperation in evil." The motive can be love or money, but we still face the question: "May I commit evil to achieve good?"

Some Famous Suicides

George Sanders, the actor, died on April 25, 1972. A Lake George, New York, newspaper quotes him as saying "Dear World. I am leaving because I am bored."

Nuland (1995) tells us of Tacitus's description of the suicide of Seneca, who after a variety of attempts was carried into a heated bath and suffocated from the steam (p. 158).

Some think the deaths of Marilyn Monroe (d. 1962) and the actor Albert Dekker (d. 1968) were not true attempts at suicide but "cries for help" that went awry. Whether or not they were "accidental" is still a matter of debate.

Nuland (1995, pp. 152-153) also relates the suicide in 1961 of the Nobel Prize-winning physicist Percy Bridgman, who at the age of 79 and in the final stages of cancer, shot himself to death in his New Hampshire home. As he got weaker, Bridgman realized the day was coming when he would not have the strength to carry out his plan. His suicide note proclaims, "It is not decent for society to make a man do this to himself. Probably, this is the last day I will be able to do it myself." In this case some friends had some advance warning.

We all know that Christianity does not approve of suicide, but again the subjective factors come into play. Somewhere along the line in my years of research, I came across this letter which some consider "famous." In February 1976, Dr. Henry Pitney Van Dusen (77) and wife Elizabeth (80) took an overdose of barbiturates in their home in Princeton, New Jersey. The Van Dusens were obviously religious people, yet they subscribed to the ethical view that the end and the intention justified the act.

To All Friends and Relations:

We hope that you will understand what we have done even though some of you will disapprove of it and some be disillusioned by it.

We have both had very full and satisfying lives. Pitney has worked hard and with great dedication for the church. I have had an adventurous and happy life. We have both had happy lives and our children have crowned this happiness.

But since Pitney had his stroke five years ago, we have not been able to do any of the things we want to do and were able to do, and my arthritis is much worse.

There are too many helpless old people who without modern medical care would have died, and we feel God would have allowed them to die when their time had come.

Nowadays it is difficult to die. We feel that this way we are taking will become more usual and acceptable as the years pass.

Of course the thought of our children and grandchildren makes us sad, but we still feel that this is the best way and the right way to go. We are both increasingly weak and unwell and who would want to die in a nursing home.

We are not afraid to die.

We send you all our love and gratitude for your wonderful support and friendship.

"O Lamb of God that takest away the sins of the world, have mercy on us.

O Lamb of God that takest away the sins of the world, grant us thy peace."

Sincerely,
Elizabeth B. Van Dusen
Henry P. Van Dusen

EUTHANASIA

The word "euthanasia" itself means "easy death," which unfortunately is not always the case. An overdose of morphine ("direct" euthanasia) would probably fit the term, but this would amount to murder, which of course is a violation of the moral and civil laws. Clergy who are aware that this is being planned will have to wrestle with their conscience on what to advise or what action to take.

The more common problem involves placing someone on a life-support system then making the decision to separate him or her from the system ("indirect" euthanasia). This can begin with the decision to place a DNR (do not resuscitate) notification on a hospital patient's chart.

Some practical considerations:

1. Is the patient at all cognizant of what is happening?
2. Is the patient in a coma? A "deep" coma?
3. What do the doctors say about the possibility of the patient's coming out of the coma?
4. If consciousness should return, what are the chances for a return to a "quality" life, and what degree of "quality"?
5. Did the patient make out an advanced directive—the so-called "living will"? Will the close relatives and the hospital honor the instructions in the directive?
6. What is the belief of the patient and close relatives about God, the soul, and the continuation of life after death in God's presence?

SOME PHILOSOPHICAL CONSIDERATIONS

Clergy being questioned by family members might discuss human life itself. Is human life an absolute value, something of such great worth that it should be maintained no matter what the situation? Or is it a "relative" value—while intrinsically of great worth, something that also has extrinsic worth? Will the patient's life be free from intractable pain? Does he have an awareness of his surroundings and even of himself? What will her physical condition be if somehow her life can be artificially continued?

What all of this comes down to is the question: Is death necessarily an evil? I personally don't think it is in some cases. Even if there were no such state of being as an afterlife, I think many of us would prefer nothingness to the kind of "life" some people must endure.

Nevertheless, as sympathetic as we all may be to those who are suffering (including Kevorkian's "patients"), counselors must tread carefully in these matters. There is an ethical question here, and the danger of scandal. Any extended conversation could include reflection upon the mystery of suffering, what possible purpose it might serve, God's love for us, and a courageous effort to embrace Christ's words from the cross: "Not my will but Thine be done."

One hopeful sign is that the medical profession is increasingly aware that as more measures become available to prolong "life," the problem of pain control must be addressed more intensively than in the past. This leads us (following Supplementary Texts on suicide and euthanasia) to Appendix II—palliative care of the dying as achieved in the hospice movement.

SUPPLEMENTARY TEXTS

Emile Durkheim: *Suicide* (1897)

Durkheim was a leading "modern" French sociologist and professor of sociology at the Sorbonne. His distinctions of the three types of suicide (egoistic, altruistic, anomic) are often quoted in the suicide literature.

> Suicide varies inversely with the degree of integration of religious . . . domestic . . . political society . . . social groups of which the individual forms a part.

Durkheim goes on to distinguish three types of suicide: egoistic, altruistic, and anomic.

In the case of egoistic (ego-Latin for self) life has lost its tranquility (as the stoics would say), nothing is left to justify "life's trials." Durkheim puts this down to "excessive individualism."

Altruistic suicide stems from some sense of "duty" or "honor" which relates to the society or a group. (One could give the Japanese "kamikaze" pilots as an example of this.)

By "anomic" Durkheim means suicides caused by a problem in the general society. He uses the examples of "financial crisis" and a mounting divorce rate. With regard to the latter he cites a study previous to his (1882) which showed that in Europe, at least, the "number of suicides" varied with that of "divorces and separations."

See also Alvarez's reading on anomic suicide below.

A. Alvarez: *The Savage God* (1972)

Having survived suicidal considerations himself, Alvarez went on to develop Durkheim's thought. His work appears in almost every bibliography on suicide.

FALLACIES

No one ever lacks a good reason for suicide.
Cesare Pavese.

> Suicide is still suspect, but the last eighty-odd years a change of tone has taken place: odium, like patriotism, is no longer enough. The suicide prejudice continues, but the religious principles by which it was once dignified now seem altogether less self-evident. As a result, the note of righteous denunciation has modified. What was once a mortal sin has now become a private vice, another "dirty little secret," something shameful to be avoided and tidied away, unmentionable and faintly salacious, less self-slaughter than self-abuse.

. . . It used to be thought, for example, that suicide as inextricably mixed with young love. . . . Yet statistically . . . [the] incidence of successful suicide, rises with age and reaches its peak between the ages of fifty-five and sixty-five. In comparison, the young are great attempters: their peak is between twenty-five and forty-four.

Romeo and Juliet also embody another popular misconception: that of the suicidal great passion. It seems that those who die for love usually do so by mistake and ill luck. It is said that the London police can always distinguish among the corpses fished out of the Thames, between those who have drowned themselves because of unhappy love affairs and those drowned for debt. The fingers of the lovers are almost invariably lacerated by their attempts to save themselves by clinging to the piers of the bridges. In contrast, the debtors apparently go down like slabs of concrete, without a struggle and without afterthought.

The third fallacy is that suicide is produced by bad weather.

The fourth fallacy is that of suicide as a national habit. Two hundred years ago, self-murder was regarded as an English sickness.

Only one generalization is wholly certain and generally agreed upon: that the official statistics reflect at best only a fraction of the real figures, which various authorities reckon to be anything between a quarter and half as large again. Religious and bureaucratic prejudices, family sensitivity, . . . personal, official and traditional unwillingness to recognize the act for what it is—all help to pervert and diminish our knowledge of the extent to which suicide pervades society.

. . . For suicide is, after all, the result of a choice. However impulsive the action and confused the motives, the moment when a man finally decides to take his own life he achieves a certain temporary clarity. Suicide may be a declaration of bankruptcy which passes judgment on a life as one long history of failures. But it is a history which also amounts at least to this one decision which, by its very finality, is not wholly a failure.

The cold-bath-laxative-and-prayer school is with us still in the shape of the two most sturdy fallacies: that those who threaten to kill themselves never do; that those who have attempted once never try again. Both beliefs are false. Stengel estimates that 75 percent of successful and would-be suicides give clear warning of their intentions beforehand, and are often driven to the act because their warnings are ignored or brushed aside. . . . At a certain point of despair a man will kill himself in order to show he is serious. It is also estimated that a person who has once been to the brink is perhaps three times more likely to go there again than someone who has not. Suicide is like diving off a high board: the first time is the worst.

All these six fallacies still prevail, despite experience, despite statistics, despite our increased sensitivity to the deviousness of human behavior and our awareness of the psyche's defenses. All these comforting fallacies have been disproved patiently and meticulously, by research.

In part, this is the doing of the great sociologist Emile Durkheim. In his battle to pierce the defenses of moral indignation which surrounded suicide, making it irrational and undiscussable, he insisted that every suicide could be classified scientifically as one of three general types—egotistic, altruistic, anomic—and that each type was the product of a specific social situation. Thus egoistic suicide occurs when the individual is not properly integrated into society but is, instead, thrown onto his own resources. Hence Protestantism, with its emphasis on free will and grace, tends to encourage suicide more than the Catholic Church. . . . Hence, too the old pattern of family life—grandparents, parents and children all living intensely together under one roof—protected each member from his impulses to self-destruction, whereas the modern disintegration of family life—children scattered, parents divorced—encourages them.

The exact opposite of all this is "altruistic suicide." It occurs when an individual is so completely absorbed in the group that its goals and its identity become his. . . . Altruistic suicide, Durkheim thought, was a characteristic of primitive societies and such primitive, rigidly structured groups as survive today, like the army. Camus summed it up early in a parenthesis: "What is called reason for living is also an excellent reason for dying."

Both egoistic and altruistic suicide are related to the degree to which the individual is integrated in his society, too little or too much. Anomic suicide, on the other hand, is the result of a change in a man's social position so sudden that he is unable to cope with his new situation. Great, unexpected wealth or great, unexpected poverty—a big win on the pools or a stock-market crash—a searing divorce or even a death in the family can thrust a man into a world where his old habits are no longer adequate, his old needs no longer satisfied.

The broad effect of Durkheim's masterpiece was to insist that suicide was not an irredeemable moral crime but a fact of society, . . . it had social causes which were subject to discernible laws and could be discussed and analyzed rationally (pp. 79-93).*

*Reprinted with permission of Gillon Aitken Associates, London.

Christopher Lukas and Henry M. Seiden:
Silent Grief: Living in the Wake of Suicide (1987)

Christopher Lukas is a writer and television director who was moved to write this book by multiple suicides in his own family. Henry Seiden is a clinical psychologist and psychotherapist. He has been a professor, a lecturer, and an administrator of a mental health facility, while holding down a practice in Forest Hills and Manhattan.

> Some of the survivors' emotional reactions are short-term, others go on for years. Some never get shaken, so fierce are the reverberations of suicide. No wonder, then, that under the pressure of this kind of stress, the lives of survivors take on new shapes and forms.

> #### Scapegoating
> In some instances of a normal death, e.g., from disease, survivors might tend to deal with their grief by blaming the deceased for dying. The suicide might also become the focus of anger of a survivor. On the other hand, a survivor might also concentrate on someone who they feel should have seen the signs of despair and anticipated a tragic result.

> #### Period of Mourning
> Survivors might also feel that the length of the mourning period will indicate the depth of the grief itself. This would especially be true if they are having trouble normalizing their lives.

> #### Guilt
> If the survivors direct feelings of guilt toward themselves they could end up not only with psychological problems but physical as well.

Our authors tell us that these are a kind of bargaining in which the survivors try to get themselves in a better "emotional position."

Our authors urge survivors to make every attempt to keep their life together, be it family or marriages or even sexual desire. They should even be on the alert that they themselves do not become victims of this act.

APPENDIX II
The Hospice Movement

"Our Lords the Sick": it is recorded that the Knights Hospitalers of St. John on the islands of Rhodes and Malta used this expression in the Middle Ages. Monasteries in England and Europe were also involved in the care of the sick.

Until recent years, people with serious, terminal illnesses usually were taken to the hospital and died there. Of course, the main purpose of the hospital is to provide specialized or high-tech care that cannot be given at home, hopefully to cure people and send them home.

I believe that nuns experimented with the "hospice concept" in Ireland early in this century, and in 1967 Dr. Cicely Saunders founded St. Christopher's Hospice in London. The Connecticut Hospice in New Haven, founded in 1971, was the first in the United States.

"Hospice" is a concept, not a place. Its purpose is to give palliative care to the dying, to make dying, if possible, somewhat easier for patients and their families. While the hospice *could* be located in a specific place or in a section of a hospital, the emphasis is on *home care* whenever the facilities of an intensive care unit are not required.

Hospice deals only with the dying. Some hospices might not get involved in a case unless the prognosis is death within three weeks. Unlike hospital staff, hospice personnel will do follow-up bereavement counseling for 13 months.

Again, the main purpose of hospice is palliative care at home. This includes control of pain in such a way that patients stay alert and cognizant of their surroundings—aware of family members, pets, visitors, and so forth. Control of pain is achieved by "heading it off" if possible, not letting it get a firm grip on the patient. The patient might be taught to use a morphine pump; some patients might use a "patch." Family members are trained how to help the hospice team.

The hospice team includes the following:

1. a visiting nurse, backed up by
2. a medical doctor;
3. a psychological counselor;
4. a "chaplain," usually from the regular clergy, for spiritual needs (one speaker in my Philosophy of Death course was a "permanent" deacon of a Catholic diocese in New Jersey); and
5. some health aides and social workers.

According to one of our course speakers, 5 to 10 percent of hospice patients are pediatric patients; most hospice patients are dying of cancer or AIDS.

Again, not everyone "qualifies" for hospice care; this depends on their condition or circumstances at home, such as whether they have family members capable of giving assistance. Financing care might not be too difficult because H.M.O.s, Medicare, and Medicaid will help with the cost.

Hospice presents an excellent opportunity for volunteerism of parishioners, students, and, of course, clergy. Back-up funds are always needed and therefore the hospice movement represents a most worthy charity. As of now, there are 2000 hospices in the United States.

The Funeral Director

Euphemisms abound in the area of death. Many people can't seem to use the term "died," so we have "passed away" or simply "passed." A textbook I once used had over 40 other words for "died": some were even rather humorous.

The "funeral director" has replaced the undertaker or mortician of yesteryear, and since "funeral director" is an all-encompassing term, I will use it here.

A "director" does many things himself or herself, but also assigns many tasks. The modern funeral has become highly complex, and survivors must first decide which funeral home to use. One funeral director told my class that people might contact clergy for advice on this matter, so some information and practical considerations are in order here.

The funeral has several purposes:

1. Hygiene: embalming prevents any danger of spread of hepatitis or tuberculosis. If there is to be a "viewing" (another term for "wake"), state law might require this procedure. It may not be required if there is to be cremation or direct, immediate burial. Clergy and others should take precautions in the presence of a dead body not yet embalmed after 48 hours.
2. Preparation for burial by taking care of the newspaper obituary and cemetery details.[1]
3. Assistance in the grieving process by allowing the family to truly realize that a death has taken place and that this death has affected many other people as well as themselves.

[1] Some ask: why a vault? The reason always given to me is the leveling of the earth over the grave. After burial the earth settles, and some coffins begin to disintegrate after a time.

Funeral home personnel can help the family in many different ways, including payment of expenses, such as for pall bearers, until life insurance claims are settled.

Funeral expenses can be prepaid, but this should be done through a reputable insurance company, not through a funeral home. (Some go out of business.)

The funeral director can deal with clergy and arrange for services either at a place of worship or at the funeral home itself. Wakes in a private home are now discouraged because of practical problems, such as steps or parking difficulties.

The question often arises whether children should be brought to the wake or to view an open coffin. Some psychologists think that children who so wish should be allowed to attend. Children frequently play or "hang out" in another room and show little emotion. Questions will come later. Ultimately, parents should make the decision. (We took our six-year-old daughter to the wake of my uncle. She saw the open casket at the end of a long room and asked, "Is Uncle Frank in that room?" I answered, "Well, in a way he is and in another way he isn't." This answer satisfied her.)

A few final words. It would behoove clergy to acquaint themselves with all local funeral homes—their reputations, directors, personnel, and facilities.[2] Anyone who cares to learn more about the funeral business should do what some of my students did for their term paper: make an appointment with a funeral director for an interview. (Others did the same with hospice personnel.)

The funeral experience, if sensitively and efficiently done, can help soften the blow of a death, at least to some degree.

[2] Because of various difficulties involved with embalming such as costs, new health codes, or the availability of good embalmers, facilities external to the funeral home have taken over this function in some places.

Conclusion

As I edited and fine-tuned this book, I kept toying with the idea of changing its focus or intent. After finishing chapter 3 I thought perhaps I should turn it into a textbook. Naturally, it would then have had a different audience. Chapters 1 and 2 suggest use as a more scholarly work. However, after writing Chapter 4 I concluded that the primary purpose should remain—a manual for clergy and counselors, if not all persons, who must deal, in whatever manner, with death and those who are left behind.

I think this book makes clear that those facing death and those who will soon be grieving for their loss must find some way to acclimate themselves to this new situation. Many of those who do not believe in God or an afterlife try to face death bravely and stoically. I have considered a small percentage of them. One wonders whether their bravado is authentic, is their acceptance of the inevitable more praiseworthy than that of some theists who mourn as if there were no God of love?

Those who reflect on the subject of death and bereavement, be they professionals or not, usually consider the consolation value of continued life. In the last two funeral homilies I have heard, the speakers concentrated on the belief that we will all meet again. I have alluded to this throughout my book. However, I imagine that for many people, in the back of their mind they worry over questions (or ignorance) about the exact nature of the next life. Will we be so overwhelmed by and subsumed within the presence of God that we really won't care about reuniting with deceased relations and friends? Can the next life in any way continue or duplicate the kind of relationship we had here on earth? What if we don't really want to be reunited with anybody? What if someone who believes in Hell has strong suspicions that a loved one did not "make it" to God's presence, in spite of the teachings on God's "infinite mercy"? Oblivion might be a preferable belief. In other words, perhaps we should rethink or readjust our use of the concept of "reunion" as a consoling factor. I do not mean discard it, but rather simply lower the level of concentration on it.

Where does this leave us? Certainly in our grief period we can turn to Divine Revelation and reflect on the redemptive sufferings of Jesus and the assurance of God Himself, given to Job, that He knows what He's doing: "Where were you when I laid the foundation—of the earth?" (38:4). "Have the gates of death been revealed to you?" (38:17).

Returning to the philosophical, the arena of reason, let me simply convey a general impression garnered from my research: first and second level philosophers, philosophers of different persuasions, even famous logicians such as Karl Popper (1902-1994) feel that life gets its value and meaning from the very fact that it *will* end, it *will* be taken from us.

Perhaps in addition to extolling the promise of life's continuation in a new and different "realm," we should also celebrate this life on earth whether it has been "a life fully lived or a life cut short by the ravages of incurable disease" (Cassell and Meier, 1960).

I close with the hope that this book will be helpful to at least some who must deal in whatever way with the death of a human person, and I thank once again all those who have helped me in this venture.

May Our Beloved Dead Rest in Peace

Bibliography

Alderman, Linda (1989). *Why Did Daddy Die?* Simon and Schuster (Pocket Books), New York.

Alvarez, Alfred (1972). *The Savage God,* Gillon Aitken Associates, London, England. (Original Publisher: Random House)

Aquinas, St. Thomas (1894). *Summa Theologica,* Forzani, Rome, Italy.

Augustine, St. (1950). *The City of God,* Modern Library, New York.

Brightman, Edgar (1930). *The Problem of God,* Abington Press, New York.

Buckman, Robert (1988). *I Don't Know What To Say,* Key Porter Books, Toronto, Canada.

Caine, Lynn (1988). *Being a Widow,* William Morrow Co., Inc., New York.

Camus, Albert (1955). *The Myth of Sisyphus and Other Essays,* Justin O'Brien (trans.), Knopf Publishing Co., New York.

Carr, John Dickson (1975). *The Life of Sir Arthur Conan Doyle* (2nd Edition), Vintage Books, New York.

Cassell, Christine and Meier, Diane (1990, September). Morals and Moralism in the Debate over Euthanasia and Assisted Suicide, *New England Journal of Medicine,* 323(1).

Cicero (1927). *Tusculan Disputations,* Loeb Classical Library, Harvard University Press, Cambridge, Massachusetts.

Colgrove, Melba, Bloomfield, Harold, and McWilliams, Peter (1991). *How to Survive the Loss of a Love,* Prelude Press, California.

Curley, Terence P. (1993). *Console One Another.* Sheed and Ward, Kansas City, Missouri.

DeSpelder, Lynn Ann and Strickland, Albert Lee (1996). *The Last Dance* (4th Edition), Mayfield, Mountain View, California.

Doka, Kenneth J. and Morgan, John D. (1993). *Death and Spirituality,* Baywood, Amityville, New York. (Part of the Death, Value and Meaning series, edited by John D. Morgan.)

Doka, Kenneth J. (1995). Friends, Teachers, Movie Stars: The Disenfranchised Grief of Children, in *Bereaved Children and Teens,* E. Grollman (Ed.), Beacon Press, Boston.

Doyle, Arthur Conan (1921). *The Wanderings of a Spiritualist,* Ronin, California.

Doyle, Arthur Conan (1930). *The Edge of the Unknown,* G. P. Putnam and Sons, London/New York.

Ducasse, Curt (1961). *A Critical Examination of the Belief in a Life After Death,* Charles C. Thomas, Springfield, Illinois.

Ducasse, Curt. *Is a Life After Death Possible,* May 1974 Lecture, University of California Press.

Durkheim, Emile (1951). *Suicide,* The Free Press (Division of Simon & Schuster), New York.

Eddington, Arthur (1939/1958). *The Philosophy of Physical Science,* University of Michigan Press, Ann Arbor, Michigan.

Eliade, Mircea (1954). *The Myth of Eternal Return,* Wm. R. Trash (trans. from French), Pantheon Books, New York.

Fingarette, Herbert (1996). *Death-Philosophical Soundings.* Open Court, Peru, Illinois.

Fitzgerald, Edward (Trans.) (1899). *Rubaiyat (of Omar Khayyam).* Garden City Books, New York (1952).

Frankl, Viktor (1959). *Man's Search for Meaning,* Simon and Schuster, New York.

Freud, Sigmund (1915). *Thoughts for the Times on War and Death,* A. A. Brill (trans.), Moffat Yard and Company, New York.

Fuccile, Dominic (1999, June 12-13). A Pastor Expresses His Grief, *Newsletter from Immaculate Heart of Mary Church,* Maplewood, New Jersey.

Gardeil, H. D. (1956). *Introduction to the Philosophy of St. Thomas Aquinas,* Vol. III, *Psychology,* B. Herder Book Co., Missouri. (Trans. by John Otto from the 1953 edition titled: *Initiation a la Philosophie de S. Thomas d'Aquin,* Vol. III, *Psychologie*).

Grollman, Earl (Ed.), (1995). *Bereaved Children and Teens,* Beacon Press, Boston.

Heidegger, Martin (1953). *An Introduction to Metaphysics,* Doubleday (Anchor Books), Garden City, New York.

Heidegger, Martin (1962). *Being and Time,* Harper and Row, New York. (Trans. by John Macquarrie and Edw. Robinson from the original *Sein und Zeit*).

Hemingway, Ernest (1953). *A Farewell to Arms,* Scribner, New York.

Hemingway, Ernest (1940). *For Whom the Bell Tolls,* C. Scribner's Sons, New York.

Hemingway, Ernest (1926/1954). *The Sun Also Rises,* C. Scribner's Sons, New York.

Hemingway, Ernest (1952). *The Old Man and the Sea,* C. Scribner's Sons, New York.

Hick, John (1978). *Evil and the God of Love,* Harper and Row, New York.

Hotchner, A. E. (1966). *Papa Hemingway,* Random House, New York.

Ionesco, Eugene (1968). *The Fragments of a Journal,* Grove Press, Inc., New York.

James, William (1955). *Pragmatism and Four Essays from the Meaning of Truth,* Meridian Books, New York. (Originally published as *Pragmatism* in 1907.)

James, William (1986). *A Pluralistic Universe,* Longmans & Green, London.

James, William (1961). *The Varieties of Religious Experience,* Collier Books, New York.

James, William and Price, Harry (1975). *Fifty Years of Psychical Research—A Critical Survey,* Arno Press (now Ayer Press), Manchester, New Hampshire.

Jeans, James (1942). *Physics and Philosophy,* Cambridge University Press, England.

Kant, Immanuel (1788/1949). *Critique of Practical Reason,* Modern Library Edition, New York.

Kavanaugh, Robert (1972). *Facing Death,* Nash Publishing (Penguin), New York.

Kübler-Ross, Elisabeth (1969). *On Death and Dying,* Macmillan, New York.

Kübler-Ross, Elisabeth (1974). *Questions and Answers on Death and Dying,* Collier/Macmillan, New York.

Kübler-Ross, Elisabeth (1983). *On Children and Death,* Macmillan, New York (now Pearson Publishing Co., Upper Saddle River, New Jersey).

Kübler-Ross, Elisabeth (1997). *The Wheel of Life,* Scribner, New York.

Kushner, Harold (1981). *When Bad Things Happen to Good People,* Avon, New York.

Lamont, Corliss (1949/96). *The Philosophy of Humanism,* Continuum Publishing Co., New York.

Lamont, Corliss (1967). "The Crisis Called Death," *The Humanist,* Vol. XXVII, No. 1, Jan/Feb.

Lewis, C. S. (1962). *The Problem of Pain,* Macmillan, New York.

Lord Tennyson, Alfred (1850). *In Memoriam,* Macdonald, London.

Lukas, Christopher and Seiden, Henry (1987). *Silent Grief: Living in the Wake of Suicide,* Scribner/Macmillan, New York.

Maimonides, Moses (1190/1997). *The Guide for the Perplexed,* Philosophic Classics (2nd Edition, Vol. II, Baird and Kaufman Edition), Prentice Hall, Upper Saddle River, New Jersey.

Marcel, Gabriel (1948). *Philosophy of Existence* (Manya Harari, trans.), Hanvill Press, London, England.

Marcel, Gabriel (1933). *Le Monde Cassé* (The Broken World), Desclée de Brouwer, Paris, France.

Maritain, Jacques (1966). *Challenges and Renewals,* University of Notre Dame Press, Notre Dame, Indiana.

Mims, Cedric (1998). *When We Die,* St. Martin's Griffin, New York.

Montaigne, Michel de (1991). *The Essays of Michel de Montaigne* (M. Screech, trans.), Allen Lane–Penguin Books, London.

Moody, Raymond (1975). *Life After Life,* (Bantam) Mockingbird Books, Covington, Georgia.

Morgan, John (1995). A Philosopher Looks at Children and Death, in *Bereaved Children and Teens,* E. Grollman (Ed.), Beacon Press, Boston.

Nietzsche, Friedrich (1927/1954). *Ecce Homo,* The Modern Library, New York. (Originally written in 1888.)

Nietzsche, Friedrich (1927/1954). *Thus Spake Zarathustra,* The Modern Library, New York. (Originally written in 1881.)

Nietzsche, Friedrich (1960). *Joyful Wisdom* (T. C. Paltry, trans.), F. Ungar, New York.

Nuland, Sherwin B. (1995). *How We Die,* Random House, Inc., New York.

O'Connor, David (1998). *God and Inscrutable Evil,* Rowman and Littlefield, New York.

O'Connor, David (1991). Swinburne on Natural Evil from Natural Processes, *International Journal for the Philosophy of Religion, 30,* 77-89.

O'Connor, David (1983). Swinburne on Natural Evil, *Religious Studies, 19,* 65-75.

Osis, Karlis and Haraldsson, Erlendur (1977). *At the Hour of Death,* Avon Books, New York.

Pascal, Blaise (1670/1995). *Pensees,* Oxford University Press, Oxford, England. (Originally published in 1670.)

Peale, Norman Vincent (1954). *The Power of Positive Thinking for Young People,* Prentice Hall, New York.

Peale, Norman Vincent (1982). *Faith is the Answer,* Ballantine, New York.

Peirce, Charles Sanders (1931). *The Collected Papers of Charles Sanders Peirce,* 8 Volumes (Hartshorne and Weiss, ed. 1981), Harvard University Press.

Price, Harry (1975). *Fifty Years of Psychical Research—A Critical Survey,* Arno Press (now Ayer Press), Manchester, New Hampshire.

Rashdall, Hastings (1907). *The Theory of Good and Evil,* Oxford University Press, London, England.

Rhine, Joseph Banks (1965). *Parasychology—From Duke to FRNM,* Parasychology Press, Durham, North Carolina.

Rhine, Joseph Banks (1956, June), Research on Spirit Survival Re-examined, *Journal of Parasychology, 20:*2, 123-126, Durham, North Carolina.

Rhine, Louisa (1981). *The Invisible Pictures,* McFarland Publishing Co., Jefferson, North Carolina.

Rivers, Joan (1997). *Bouncing Back,* HarperCollins, New York.

Royce, Josiah (1898). *Studies of Good and Evil,* D. Appleton, New York.

Sabom, Michael (1981). *Recollections of Death: A Medical Investigation,* Harper and Row, New York.

Sartre, Jean-Paul (1947). *Existentialism is a Humanism,* Philosophical Library, New York.

Sartre, Jean-Paul (1956). *Being and Nothingness,* Philosophical Library, New York.

Sartre, Jean-Paul (1953). *Existential Psychoanalysis* (Hazel Barnes, trans.), Philosophical Library Inc., New York.

Schopenhauer, Arthur (1928). *Metaphysics of Love and the Sexes,* Modern Library, New York.

Schopenhauer, Arthur (1818). *The World as Will and Idea,* Vol. I (10th Edition, 1957), Routledge & Kegan Paul, London, England.

Smith, Huston (1958). *The Religions of Man,* Harper and Row, New York.

St. Vincent Millay, Edna (1928). *The Buck in the Snow and Other Poems,* Harper and Brothers, New York

Swinburne, Richard (1996). *Is There a God,* Oxford University Press, New York.

Wells, Rosemary (1998). *Helping Children Cope with Grief,* Sheldon Press, London, England.

Vaux, Kenneth (1992). *Death Ethics,* Trinity Press International, Philadelphia, Pennsylvania.

"Parting" (Dickinson), 42
Pascal, Blaise, 28
"Pastor Expresses His Grief, A"
    (Fuccile), 73
Peale, Norman V., 50–51
Peirce, Charles S., 10, 30–31
Pensées (Pascal), 28
Phaedo (Plato), 10
"*Philosopher Looks at Children and
    Death, A*" (Morgan), 61
Philosophers/writers, reflections of
  atheists/agnostics, 34–38
  defining what a philosopher is,
      25–26
  novelists/poets/other writers,
      41–53
  pagans, 38–41
  secular, 23–24
  theistic, 21–23, 26–34
  value in the end of living, 88
Philosophy of Existence (Marcel),
    33–34
Philosophy of Humanism (Lamont),
    38
Philosophy of Physical Science
    (Eddington), 11
Physical evil, 16, 18
Physics and Philosophy (Jeans), 10
Plato, 10, 38
Platonists/Aristotelians and
    immortality, 6
Pluralistic Universe (James), 23
Poets, 41–43, 46, 48–53
Popper, Karl, 88
Power of Positive Thinking (Peale),
    50
*Pragmatism and Four Essays on
    Truth* (James), 31
Precognition, 7
Price, Harry, 11
Problem of God (Brightman), 23
Problem of Pain (Lewis), 24

*Questions and Answers on Death
    and Dying* (Kübler-Ross),
    47

Rashdall, Hastings, 32
Rational argument and immortality,
    6
Reactive grief, 55
Recollections of Death (Sabom), 8
Reincarnation, 14
  See also Immortality, human
Religious Man (Smith), 21–22
Remarriage, 58
Resolution stage in grieving process,
    66
Reunion concept, rethinking use of,
    87–88
Rhine, Joseph B., 7, 12
Rhine, Louisa, 7, 12–13
Rocchi, Frank, 73
Roman Ritual, 8
Royce, Josiah, 24
Rubaiyat (Khayyam), 46
Russell, Bertrand, 36

Sartre, Jean-Paul, 37
Saunders, Cicely, 83
Savage God (Alvarez), 79–81
Schopenhauer, Arthur, 29
Seattle (Chief), 40–41
Secular philosophers, 23–24
Seiden, Henry, 82
Seneca, 75
Sermons on dying/death, 2–3
Seton Hall University, 16
Shakespeare, William, 51
"Ship of Death" (Lawrence), 48–49
Shock/disorganization, grief and,
    55
Sibling, death of a, 59–60, 62–64
SIDS (sudden infant death
    syndrome), 59
*Silent Grief: Living in the Wake of
    Suicide* (Lukas & Seiden), 82
Sleepless in Seattle, 58
Smith, Huston, 21–22
Socrates, 5, 38
Soft determinism, 75
Soul
  arguments concerning the
      spiritual, 6–8

[Soul]
    explaining death of a parent to
        child using the, 61–62
St. Christopher's Hospice, 83
Stevenson, Ian, 13
Stoicism
    Aurelius, Marcus, 40
    Cicero, Marcus T., 39–40
    Epictetus, 40
    Frankl, Viktor, 45
    Montaigne, Michel de, 27
Studies of Good and Evil (Royce),
    24
Sudden infant death syndrome
    (SIDS), 59
Suffering. *See* Evil and human
    suffering
Suicide
    euthanasia, 77–78
    judging those who commit,
        75–76
    philosophical considerations, 78
    Seneca, 76
    signs leading up to, 75
    soft determinism, 75
    texts, supplementary, 79–82
    Tolstoy, Leo, 53
    Van Dusen, Henry/Elizabeth,
        76–77
Suicide (Durkheim), 79
Summa contra Gentiles (Aquinas),
    27
Summa of Theology (Aquinas), 8–9,
    20, 21, 27
Sun Also Rises, The (Hemingway),
    45
Swinburne, Algernon C., 51–52
Swinburne, Richard, 22–23
Synechism, 10

Tacitus, 76
Tennyson, Alfred, 52–53
"Thanatopsis" (Bryant), 41
"Theatre of the Absurd" (Ionesco),
    45

Theistic philosophers/writers,
    21–23, 26–34
Theory of Good and Evil (Rashdall),
    32
*Thoughts for the Times on War and
    Death* (Freud), 35
Thus Spake Zarathustra
    (Nietzsche), 34
Time period, grieving process has
    no set, 56
Tolstoy, Leo, 53
"To Philosophize is to Learn to Die"
    (Montaigne), 28
Traditional approach in argu-
    ment for the spiritual soul,
    6–7
Treatise on Angels (Aquinas), 27
Tusculan Disputations (Cicero),
    39–40

University of Utrecht, 12
University of Virginia, 13

Van Dusen, Henry/Elizabeth,
    76–77
Varieties of Religious Experience
    (James), 23, 31

Wakes, speakers at, 60
Wanderings of a Spiritualist
    (Doyle), 11
War and Peace (Tolstoy), 53
Weisel, Elie, 16
Wheel of Life (Kübler-Ross), 47, 48
*When Bad Things Happen to Good
    People* (Kushner), 18
Why Did Daddy Die? (Alderman),
    71–72
Widow (Caine), 70
Wife, death of a, 57–58
World as Will and Idea
    (Schopenhauer), 29, 39
"World Strangeness" (Watson),
    50–51